ROCKS FOR FAMILIES

Dr. Rick Janelle

Dr. Rick Janelle

24 Flint Ridge Dr.

Reading, PA 19607

www.rickjanelle.com

Original cover design by Ed Burns, Jr., Melior Marketing; revised by Velvet Hall, Merkle

ISBN: 978-1-7332009-1-2

Dedication

WITH MUCH LOVE AND THANKFULNESS

This book is dedicated to:

My wife, Tammy L. Janelle
And my 4 delightful kids

*May we always be
deeply involved in each other's lives,
both in this world and the one to come.*

Table of Contents

ROCKS FOR FAMILIES

"There are no guarantees that good parents will always produce good children.

However, the odds are in favor of those who wisely examine themselves and the environment they are producing for those children."

-Dr. Rick Janelle

What's Missing at the Heart of Our Homes?

In my studies about what others are doing to teach Judeo-Christian values about the family, I've found that there are too few sites and people who are promoting what I think is the most important thing about Christian parenting. You look at most of these books, classes, websites — some of them are free, some of them you pay for — and almost all of them boil down to this premise: "*If you do things exactly as we say, you'll raise good kids and be a successful parent.*"

The problem is that real life doesn't work that way, nor is it what the Bible teaches. With that in mind, I wrote this book to share my views.

I think that there's something wrong at the root of many of our homes.

You get to be the ultimate judge for your own life and your own family, of course, but I hope that you will hear me out. If you think I am wrong, feel free to correct me.

I believe that there are two basic ways of looking at raising and leading a family: *what we do* versus *who we are*. Though the distinction seems small, it is anything but. It's the difference between *getting our kids to behave* versus *being godly parents.* The former is focused on doing the correct thing in the correct order and getting them to do the correct thing when we want them to. The latter is focused on looking in the mirror and making sure that who we are is a functioning, healthy person for them to follow in the first place.

Which do you think is easier? Which do you think most people are more interested in doing?

Don't get me wrong, I believe in having kids that behave and function well. I also believe that managing our families and our households well is an underlying, defining characteristic of ALL God's people (not just church leaders).

But that's not my point.

My point is that being able to do all that is so much easier if you are taking care of your internal values instead of merely focusing on your outwardly apparent values. With that in mind, let's review some introductory points.

Proverb or Promise?

Here's a warning for parents and grandparents. There are no guarantees that good parents will always produce good kids.

Anytime I've taught this, there is almost always someone who speaks up and says, "But I've always heard the Biblical proverb, 'Train up a child in the way he should go and when he's old, he won't depart from it' *(Proverbs 22:6)*.

I've heard that verse used many times to beat people over the head, and there's no need for it. Why? It's a proverb. Not a promise.

What I mean is, the Bible is not a single book. It's a library of books. There are 66 books in this library called "The Bible." And just like any library, the different books are written by different authors, as different kinds of literature, with different kinds of purposes, for different kinds of audiences, and with different kinds of wordings.

The Book of Proverbs, one of the books within this library, is a collection of wise sayings from the day of King Solomon and before. He wanted to bring wise sayings together that would teach young people the best way to stack the deck of life in favor of their success. Solomon didn't just think up all these pithy sayings. He collected them like some people collect stamps or model cars or whatever they collect. And one of those sayings just happens to be translated into English as, "Train up a child in the way he should go and when he's old, he won't depart from it." It is a concise statement of how things generally work.

Is this particular proverb generally true? Yes. Generally speaking, if children are reared with fore-thought, consistency, and with a habit of practicing sound, long-term goals, they more often than not turn out better than those who aren't reared that way.

But one of the interesting things when you study Biblical proverbs is that there are many places where two proverbs take the opposite positions. If you're viewing them as promises, it's easy to decide that the Bible contradicts itself.

Here's one example. "Don't answer a fool according to his folly" *(Proverbs 26:4)*. Just one verse later it says, "Answer a fool according to his folly" *(Proverbs 26:5)*. But which is it? If you take each proverb as a promise or guarantee, then it can get confusing.

But it's not a promise. It's not a command. It's not set in stone.

So you shouldn't beat yourself or other people over the head with this idea of, "my kids didn't turn out the way I want them to," or, "my grandkids didn't turn out the way I want them to, so I must be a horrible person." You can be a wonderful person and still have children who make bad choices. Conversely, there are many good adults that were raised in horrible living situations.

It is true that if parents are good parents and grandparents are good grandparents, the odds get shifted. The deck gets stacked in your favor. But God says that we each are responsible for our own selves. We will individually answer for the way we act, speak, and treat others. *(Ezekiel 18:4)*.

Ultimately, there's more to the equation than "Good Parenting = Good Kids."

Elements in Producing a Crop: *Matthew 13:3-9*

This is where the story from *Matthew 13* can be instructional. Here, we see a farmer who is trying to raise a good crop.

If you want a good crop, it's important to have a good farmer. Two other variables in this equation are "the seed" and "the soil." And that's true in human life as well. If you want a good crop to come from your family, you need good "farmers" (parents), good "seed" (teaching) and good "soil" (family environment).

Variables in Producing a Good Family:

The Farmer	Parents
The Seed	Teaching and/or Child
The Soil	Family Environment
"Uncontrollables"	Things and People Outside our Homes

In my view, the key ingredient to success or failure is the SOIL. In gardening, bad seed is less likely than bad soil. That's why there are entire governmental and educational agencies that focus on soil analysis. You can send a soil sample to an agricultural testing service. They will analyze what is either missing or harmful in the dirt so you can take appropriate steps to make it the best possible. If there is a problem after everything possible has been done to correct soil deficiencies, the next step is to examine the seed itself. You need to take account of your own family's "soil" and assess if there is anything you can do to improve the quality.

The Heart of the Child

The teaching and training you do can be compared to "seed" that is planted within the "soil" of a child's heart and mind. Alternatively, the individual child's heart can be viewed as the "seed" that is planted in the "soil" of the family.

Did you know that one of the things Jesus died on the cross to ensure was that every individual would have the right to choose for themselves how to live? None are forced into undesired slavery to serve God. Those who refuse to follow him have been set free from being required to follow him. In that sense, Christ set everyone free, followers and rebels alike.

Since your children have the right to choose, will they always make the right choices? In turn, I ask you, did YOU always make the right choices as you grew through the various stages of your life? Did YOU always make your parents and grandparents proud with your decisions and actions?

But being free to make bad choices, and actually making bad choices, doesn't automatically mean that all hope is lost. For every bad decision you have made, there are (hopefully) dozens of good ones to counteract it. The trick is giving your children the best chance of overcoming their bad decisions.

The Soil

Just as teaching and training take root in the "soil" of a child's heart and mind, the family unit also can be illustrated as "soil" that a "crop" of children grow from. This is a major factor in rearing good offspring. In many ways, the "soil" we provide is the most important variable.

Fortunately, it's also the component that we have the most control over. Parents run into serious problems when kids can't hear what parents say because the parent's actions shout so loudly.

And so, we need to remember some things. God's goal for our kids is that they be godly offspring. I think that we're making a HUGE mistake if we lose sight of that. One of the biggest mistakes we can make is to believe that our number one parenting goals are that our kids be richer, more educated, and healthier than we were. While those are admirable goals to have, they should not be number one.

Our goal for raising kids is not to give them everything they want. It's not to keep them out of trouble. It's not to make sure they have the newest clothes, and the finest shoes. Should we do those things if we can? Yes. If we can and want to, it's perfectly ok to do so. But that's not the main point.

The end-goal should be neither prosperity, nor safety, nor ease of life. I know people whose entire family life revolves around the idea of "keeping my kids safe, happy and carefree," and they wonder why one of their kids rebels. One becomes a Navy SEAL. The other becomes so afraid or non-functioning that they get hooked on drugs. Yet another sits in mom's basement biting his or her nails because they're afraid to go to school or get a job. All because we didn't keep the main thing the main thing.

Some people say, "I don't want my kids to get hurt." Me neither. But answer this: Where and when did YOU learn the best, most helpful things in YOUR life? When it was easy, or when it was really hard? Just as God allows us to make mistakes, so we too must let our children weather a few storms.

The bottom line is, anyone helping to raise that child needs to come to an agreement about the core values your family finds most important. Once you have determined the best "soil," you need to stick to that shared vision. If you can't come to an agreement on this, then it is very unlikely that the "soil" you produce will provide a nurturing environment for your "crop" of children.

Uncontrollable Influences

Unfortunately, uncontrollable influences can overcome even the best of seeds planted in the richest soil.

I grew up in North Texas where there's seemingly endless flat farmland that goes on for miles. It takes big, huge tractors to work the fields. When I was a boy, there were years that the farmers did everything right. They had the perfect seed. The ground was well prepared. They had all the weeds killed. They kept it cultivated perfectly. And despite all of that effort and preparation, sometimes the sky would turn dark, and boiling black clouds would come rolling across the plains bringing a hailstorm that beat all the plants into the dirt.

Whose fault was that? Was it a bad farmer? Was it bad seed? Was it bad soil? No. Sometimes the crops got hailed out. Sometimes things like this happen to the "crops" of our lives. That's when many find that their Christian faith is challenged the most.

Sometimes things like that happen within even the best of families. So when you see a family where there are good parents/grandparents but a rebellious kid, don't automatically assume that the problem is or was the parents. Maybe it was poor parenting, but maybe it wasn't.

Our Job vs. God's Job

Whether you're talking about a wheat field or a family, there are things that are clearly outside of our ability to control. These are the things we need to leave to God's management. It's God's job to deal with the nature of the seed and its growth. It's God's job to deal with uncontrollable influences. And, ultimately, it's God's job to deal with our individual children and the choices they make.

But there ARE things within our control, and we should be extremely conscientious about how seriously we take care of our part. We're responsible for producing offspring. And it's our job to provide the best possible soil for their maximum growth and achievement.

What the Bible Says About These Things:

God's Job	Dealing with the nature of the seed and its growth	*1 Corinthians 3:6*
God's Job	Dealing with outside, uncontrollable influences	*Matthew 6:25-34*
Our Job	Producing offspring	*Genesis 1:28; 8:17; 9:1; 9:7*
Our Job	Providing the best soil for maximum achievement	*Malachi 2:13-16*

Good News

I will tell you today that, out of all the mistakes a father could make, I've probably made most of them. I've always been a good guy at heart. I've tried to be a moral and ethical man, but I've made many, many, stupid mistakes with my children. I didn't always make the right choices, but God and other like-minded people helped me. It's demoralizing sometimes to remember all my own failures in dealing with my children.

But despite all the things I haven't gotten right, I've consistently tried to set the right example. Our example is the most important thing, especially when we make mistakes. How we handle failures is a crucial part of adulthood.

One of my constant prayers for my children has been, "help me to do my best, and please bring people and events into their lives to fill the holes I leave." My testimony is that God has been faithful in honoring that prayer. He has consistently worked in my kids' lives to provide those badly needed things and people. Some of the provisions have come from my own growth and efforts, and many of them have come from other people that I worked to bring into their lives.

I started praying for my children when they were very young. And today as they're all grown, and as grandchildren are coming into my life, I pray even more fervently. "God, if you need my permission to do something with them that will wake them up, you've got it. I love my children, and I want their lives to be successful. And if that means that they need to get beat up a little bit, if that means disease, pain or hardship, if that's how it has to be, then so be it. I want my children to be productive, honorable people. I know that I don't understand how all these things work, but God, you do. PLEASE work powerfully on their behalf in their lives."

I've had people tell me, "You're a horrible man for praying like that." But the bottom line is that I don't care what the price is for my children's ultimate success and well-being. I don't care if they're angry with me because other parents let their kids do things I don't.

It doesn't bother me to hear my kids say, "But, I want..." My answer to that is, "That's okay. It won't hurt you to want something." I believe that our kids need us to be their parents more than they need us to be their friends. Ultimately, I care about what is best for them in the long term, not what will make them happy in the short term.

It's God who produces good children, not us. However, he uses the good environment that we produce to change the odds for the choices that they make.

In other words, there are things we can do to make it easier for them to live well and harder for them to choose poorly. When we surround them with like-minded people (you are most likely to find them in places like healthy churches, well-run schools, and well-coached sports teams), we can work together to provide the best soil possible for their development.

To Summarize

There are multiple components to this family/farm metaphor. There's the parent/farmer, the home environment/soil, and the kid/seed. We want to stack the deck so that they've got the richest soil possible, the best seed, the least weeds, and the most fertilizer. And we hope and pray that seriously destructive things like floods, ice and hail storms stay far away from them.

If we do it well, it's easier for them to make wise choices. If we are skillful, they will need to really work hard to go the wrong direction. And, when they fail, they know how and have the strength to get up and try again. Remember, God's goal is that we raise godly offspring, not prosperity, safety, or ease of life.

So, what is my primary role as a parent? — *Preparing and maintaining that great family environment.* Now, the Bible relies on the farming metaphor, but I'd like to introduce you to another metaphor for the markers of a healthy, successful family: Rocks.

7 "Rocks" for a Healthy Family

In *Matthew 7:24-27*, Jesus described the difference between wise and foolish builders.

> "Therefore everyone who hears these words of mine and puts them into practice is like a wise man who built his house on the rock. The rain came down, the streams rose, and the winds blew and beat against that house; yet it did not fall, because it had its foundation on the rock. But everyone who hears these words of mine and does not put them into practice is like a foolish man who built his house on sand. The rain came down, the streams rose, and the winds blew and beat against that house, and it fell with a great crash."

Jesus clearly implies that there are some basic underlying principles involved in building successful lives. This is also true for the "building" of a family unit.

All around us, we can easily see various levels of success in existing families. Not getting the supporting foundation of our families right can have disastrous consequences, for ourselves and for those who live with us.

Families are not made of rocks, gravel, sand or water. Times, traditions, priorities, and personalities vary over time and across ethnicities. But I believe that, at the most basic level, there are some foundational "rocks" that all successful families tend to prioritize in the fabric of their families. I also believe that leaving any of them out, or executing any of them poorly, makes a family less stable, productive, and happy.

My purpose is not to show you how to get every detail done perfectly. Even if you are always at your best (and who could ever make that claim?), you will never be able to do everything right.

But, by getting the basic foundational things in place, and by working on them consistently, we stand a much better chance of having the success that we want.

Humans have basic needs that must be met in order to feel safe and secure. These "rocks" that I'll be addressing in my book represent the foundation for building a home where both our and our child's spiritual and emotional needs are met to their fullest potential.

Here Are My 7 Rocks for a Healthy Family:

- Rock 1: Sanctuary   Am I safe?
- Rock 2: Development   Who am I?
- Rock 3: Fences   What are the rules?
- Rock 4: Rejoicing   Am I important?

Is life good?

- Rock 5: Relationships Am I loved?
- Rock 6: Tradition   Where do I belong?
- Rock 7: Direction   Why am I here?

Where do I go?

ROCKS FOR FAMILIES

"This place, this sanctuary, that we call home should be a place that makes us feel joyful, safe, and at peace.

Let your home be a place of beauty.

Let it be that your home never makes you feel trapped, stressed, or drained. Having a place of sanctuary is very important for the mental well-being.

No matter what happens in the outside world there needs to always be a place for you to balance out and recharge."

-Avina Celeste

Rock 1: Sanctuary — Am I Safe?

In order to build a strong family, we need to make our home a place of refuge. A safe haven where we can go to rest. A place where we can feel secure and comforted.

One of my favorite pictures is a photograph by Jean Guichard, a French photographer who took the photo as part of a series in 1989. The photo, *Phares dans la Tempete, la Jument,* depicts a lighthouse keeper who looks as if he's just taking a breath of fresh air, when in reality, he's frightened and waiting for rescuers to take his colleagues and him away from the waves and life-threatening waters that have surged up all around them.

The man is standing at the door with his hand in his pocket. He's kind of slouched on one leg. The potentially deadly water is pummeling this lighthouse, and yet he looks completely unshaken. What allows him to stand there in that open door in the open air with all of that mighty power crashing around him? What allows him to be so casual and nonchalant?

When I first laid eyes on that picture, I

thought it to be a beautiful representation of what our household should be for all the members of our family (parents, kids, and grandparents too). Home should feel and look like complete calm in the midst of chaos. Let that thought sink into your mind.

We live in a world today that is much like those crashing waves, right? Our government's crazy. Our medicine is crazy. Our laws are crazy. The people driving on our freeways are crazy. The kids your children are going to school with are crazy (and their parents are too). We live in neighborhoods full of crazy people, and some days we look into the mirror and see the craziest of them all looking right back at us.

But if we make God and family our lighthouse, if we turn our home into a sanctuary, then we too will experience a sense of calm in the face of utter chaos.

5 Things to Make Your Home a Sanctuary

Safety

A house of sanctuary should be a place where your children can always run to in their times of need. I don't know how you work with your kids. But with our kids, if they're calling their mama, things are okay; they call Mom just to chat. But if my cell phone rings, and I see that it's one of my kids, I know it's a serious situation, at least to them. In my family, the kids seldom call me just to talk.

If my kids call me, it's because there's a need or a problem that they need my help with. The reason is that, from the time they were little, whatever their problems were, even if they caused it themselves, I tried not to scold them or punish them for coming to me. If they made a mistake, I would make them face and deal with the mistake, but I did my best to help them feel safe as we worked together to fix it.

Just as we should feel comfortable turning to the Lord with our problems in life, so too should our children be able to come to us for help. This doesn't mean that there won't be consequences, of course. And it absolutely does NOT mean that we never get irritated or short-tempered from some of their antics. But we should never make them feel as if they will be shunned for having made a mistake.

Acceptance

I remember one day, when our older son was in grade school. He was playing baseball with some buddies, and they broke one of the back windows in the church building. They didn't know I was watching and listening when I heard Ben's buddy say, "Oh, no, my dad's gonna kill me!"

But all Ben said was, "I bet my dad makes me fix it."

Notice the difference in their responses. My wife and I have always made it clear that, no matter what, our children will be loved and accepted. Mistakes happen. Anger rises and falls. But how we feel about our family shouldn't change.

Ben and his buddy came to my office, and he said, "Dad, we broke the window."

I said, "Yeah, I know. What are you gonna do about it?" They kind of shuffled their feet and looked at each other.

Finally, Ben looked up and said, "I guess you're gonna teach me how to fix it, right?"

"Yep. That's exactly right. Who's gonna pay for the glass?"

"I guess I'll have to somehow, right?"

See my point? If you accept your kids, you make them feel safe enough to come to you when life throws them a curveball (no pun intended). Just keep in mind that acceptance doesn't mean blind belief. It's not, "oh, my baby would never do anything like that." Your kids are your kids, but ultimately, they are exactly that: *kids*. Children can make just about any mistake at any given moment.

But, see, being a home of refuge means you make it safe to talk about things. You make home a place where you are accepting of them and the things that they get involved with. When there's a problem, you say, "Let's fix this together. I'll help you, but you're the one on the hook because you're the one who did this." Isn't that a safer, healthier approach than screaming or threatening them so much that they feel the need to keep secrets from you?

Privacy

A reasonable level of privacy goes a long way toward making your home a sanctuary for your kids. For example, it's my opinion that if children are behind a closed door, that you should knock on their door instead of just bursting in. You might say that because you pay the bills, you can do whatever you want, but if you're serious about building a family and building a safe home, then you've got to make reasonable concessions.

I think that you should give them the same courtesy you expect from them. If your bedroom door is closed, they shouldn't just come bursting in, right? So what's so wrong about returning the gesture? Later on down the line, if they abuse that right to privacy, then you make adjustments. But until they prove they can't handle being trusted, then you should give them the benefit of the doubt.

Peace

Home should be a place for jokes and laughter and enjoyment and encouragement and lifting each other up. We should look forward to being with each other. We shouldn't dread next Christmas because a certain relative is going to be there. We shouldn't come home and go straight to our rooms to avoid talking to anyone else.

Whatever you have to do to bring tranquility and harmony to your house, then you need to do that. If that means things like going to counseling, having family meetings, or attending church discussion or support groups, etc., then do it. Find what works for your family because a house without peace can never be a sanctuary.

Simplicity

Why simplicity? Because the more simple your home is, the less your family has to think about it. If you've got too many overly-complicated rules, then it makes it difficult for anyone to relax in your home. If you've got too many activities going on at once, then that can also be a problem for your family. It's one thing to pursue your interests, but it's another thing to have so many commitments pulling you in so many different directions that you can't enjoy any of your activities.

Sometimes, less is more. Figure out what your family values most, and let those values guide your home. From your rules, to your interactions with each other, to your choice in activities, remember to keep it simple.

"Sanctuary" in Scripture

Is the idea of "sanctuary" really important to God? Absolutely. The Bible tells us about "cities of refuge." They show God's concern for peace and safety, especially during times of stressful conflict.

When God was giving the people of Israel the land of Canaan, the plan was that they were going to move in, conquer this land, live in houses they didn't build, eat from gardens they didn't plant, and pick fruit from trees they hadn't taken care of and pruned. It's a tremendous offer, right?

In return, God tells them to build *cities of refuge.* He explains that each should be a place that is easily accessible, a place where if someone commits a crime by mistake, then they can find safety until they receive a trial to determine exactly what happened.

Many of our laws today are based on these and other ancient Biblical laws. By and large, the rule of the fist and the club was the primary law in those times. Revenge and punishment was the rule of the land, and the way you kept peace was through retribution. If someone killed your son, then you would kill theirs. If someone stole from you, then you would "steal" their hand.

But what God wanted was for them to make their homes and, by extension, their homeland, places where people could be at peace, even if they had done something horrible by mistake.

The Bible acknowledges the difference between "malice aforethought" and making an unintended mistake, as do the laws of our country. God understands that society can't function if revenge runs rampant and everyone lives in fear of blind retribution. He doesn't want our homes to be places where people are under stress or are always having to look over their shoulder.

Why? Because everybody makes mistakes. Inevitably, people will get hurt or hurt someone else, and if you're always afraid that somebody's going to be stabbing you in the back because of something you didn't even know you did, then you can't relax. You can't take it easy. God showed concern for people by wanting these cities of refuge.

Below are some relevant passages:

Biblical Cities of Refuge

List of cities:	*Joshua 20:7-9*
Building roads to refuge:	*Deuteronomy 19:3*
Purpose of refuge:	*Exodus 21:13-14*

These days, you can find the lingering influence of this biblical notion in the civil courts. I know a guy that almost lost his life when they were trying to pull a tractor out of a rice paddy with a chain. The chain broke, whipped around the cab of the tractor, hit him in the head, and almost killed him. Was that the fault of the guy driving the tractor? The tractor's owner? The manufacturer of the chain? The supplier of the steel for the chain's manufacturer? Things like this can and do happen, and without proper balance and guidance, the results can escalate out of control. Today, we have the court system. Back then, God had his followers create sanctuaries.

We find this idea of sanctuary in other places of scripture, as well. For example, *Proverbs 14:26* says, "Whoever fears the Lord has a secure fortress, and for their children it will be a refuge." God desires security and refuge for our families. He wants your children and grandchildren to have a place where they can kick off their shoes, lean back and relax.

Isn't that what you want? Do you really want people that you love and care about to come to your house and sit perfectly ramrod straight on the edge of their chair, eyes wide open, afraid to say something that's going to make you mad? "Y-y-y-yes sir. Yes, sir. Right away! N-n-n-no ma'am, no ma'am. No, ma'am. As you say!" Is that what you want? Because it's not what God wants. You might think you've got your family's respect, but such fear shows that all you've really got is their fear.

What God wants is places where our families can relax. There are certain homes I hate visiting because the people who live there don't understand this. They don't create a home that is a place of peace. Instead, they constantly argue, fuss, and butt heads over who's boss or who gets to have things their way.

I've known several men who make this mistake, and they ruin their own ability to enjoy life. They come home and expect to be treated like a king. They say, or at least think, "a man's a king in his own castle, and what I say goes around here. I may not be the boss at work. I may not be the boss in the government, and they may rob my taxes to pay somebody else, but, by golly, I'm in charge here."

If you order your family around, they might do it, but then you've just ruined your own home. Why? Because you've taken what should be a place of refuge, and you've turned it into something completely different. And in choosing to make your home a battleground, you are leading the future of your family down a contentious and stressful path.

Remember the story of Judas Iscariot, the man who betrayed Jesus for 30 pieces of silver? The point of Judas's tale is not merely to teach us about betrayal, but also to show us that we should be careful who we become as we pursue our goals.

There are bound to be a few battles in your home, but if you are only ever fighting for what is best for <u>you</u> as opposed to the good of your <u>family</u>, then you're going to lose the war. Plain and simple, your home will never be a place of refuge until you accept that. God knew this, and He wanted His people to strive to make their homes a shelter from the temptations and aggravations of a sinful world.

Verses on Sanctuary

- In Hebrews, Jesus is portrayed as our refuge. It says, "We do have such a high priest... who serves in the sanctuary, the true tabernacle set up by the Lord" *(Hebrews 8:1-2)*.

- Jesus said, "Take my yoke upon you and learn from me, for I am gentle and humble in heart, and you will find rest for your souls" *(Matthew 11:29)*.

- When Jesus was leaving Earth, He was talking to His disciples before His crucifixion. He said, "Don't be afraid. I'm going to prepare a place for you, and if I go and prepare a place for you, I'll come back and I'll receive you" *(John 14:1-3)*.

Conclusion

Here's my definition of a house of refuge: "a place where children are loved, helped, and kept safe." And you <u>must</u> lead by example. If they don't see Mama safe and well taken care of, then they don't feel safe either. Likewise, they need to see Daddy coming home, relaxing, and being a person that's easily approachable. Your home should be a harbor, a fortress, and a fire all in one. What's more important are the inhabitants, not the building. In other words, it's not <u>where</u> you live that makes your home a sanctuary, it's <u>how</u> you live.

The family of God works the same way. The building means nothing to God, but the people who gather there mean everything to Him. We must carefully maintain and jealously defend our houses of refuge. It's not just for the benefit of the kids either. Refuge is something that adults need, and a church where people are low-key, relaxed, and friendly makes people walk in and say, "Ah." It shouldn't matter what color your skin is; it shouldn't matter whether you have a bald head or a head full of hair; it shouldn't matter whether you are covered in tattoos or piercings. Why? Because God wants His people to have refuge.

One of the things that I talk to young ministers about is the balancing of ministry and family life. The odds are largely stacked against a preacher's kids staying faithful to God. Few stay actively involved in church once they leave home, and one of the reasons is because it's so very difficult to protect your home when you live in the glass bowl of being a minister. Your life (and by extension, your family's life) is on display at all times for others to see. Everybody (it seems) complains about your kids. Everybody watches them. Every little mistake they make, someone notices. Some people are quick to say, "oh, I knew he wasn't any good. Look at what his kid did." Every mistake gets magnified way out of control, and your kids are the center of this drama. Like the man in the lighthouse, it is all too easy to become distracted by the raging waters around you.

I was very fortunate. God gave me a wife whose father was not a minister, but who was a small town school superintendent. The politics of the jobs are very similar. Some people liked him. Some people didn't. Whatever he said, some people thought it was great, some people thought it wasn't. No matter what he did, gossip, criticism, and speculation was sure to follow.

We need to protect our family members

from this as much as possible. We don't need to allow other people, whether it's our parents or our grandparents or a neighbor or even a well-meaning (but nosey) preacher like me, to intrude too much into the sanctity of our home. Your home is your home, God holds you responsible as the head of your household for what goes on under your roof, not anyone else.

So, just to reiterate, a house of sanctuary is a place where children are loved, helped, and kept safe. It is a harbor, a fortress, and a warm fire, all in one. It is a place of acceptance. It is about the people you love, not the walls that make the building. A sanctuary like that must be carefully maintained and jealously defended. It should not be a place where you walk in to find someone shaking their finger in your face and admonishing you for not doing better or making better choices.

Maybe we find ourselves doing that in our families, or we see our homes become increasingly consumed by constant bickering and antisocial behavior. But it just seems to me that the rest of life is pretty much a dog-eat-dog world, so let's make our families different. Let's make our homes a special place to be. This is what our children desperately need from us to make our homes a true lighthouse in the storms of life.

Prayer

Father, thank you for being concerned about our safety and our sense of peace and comfort. Thank you for creating ways for the burdens of life to be lighter and to be shared so that we're not crushed under the weight of them.

We pray, God, that you would help us with our children and grandchildren to do what we can to create homes of refuge, and whether we have children or not, God, may we be hospitable people to the point that people long to come to our homes. May they see what we have in our marriages or in our families, and say, "Wow, there must be a God, and I want some of that."

Forgive us, God, for the times that we're spiteful, we're hateful, we're sharp, or we're rude with each other, whether that's in our homes, in our churches or our community. Thank you for your son, Jesus, and continue to bless us. In Christ's name we pray. Amen.

ROCKS FOR FAMILIES

Regarding the development of self-identity in the family, PBS film critic Michael Medved said,

"What matters ultimately in the culture wars is what we do in our daily lives – not the big statements that we broadcast to the world at large, but the small messages we send through our families and our neighborhoods and our communities."

-The De-Valuing of America by *William Bennett*

Rock 2: Development — Who Am I?

We need to make our homes a place of fabrication and formation. Let's say you wanted to make some pottery. Each piece of this pottery is different. You can tell where it's from by the way it's shaped and how it's painted.

One of the things that determines how it's shaped is the nature of the clay itself. For example, with ancient Greek pottery, the clay found in Attica around Athens is a stronger clay that can be stretched longer and thinner than others. The clay found around Corinth doesn't have the same tensile strength. Its final shape has to be blockier and bulkier, or it will fall apart in the kiln.

One of the ways you can tell the difference between pottery that was made in Athens and pottery that was made in Corinth is that Corinthian pottery has a chunky, heavy duty look to it, whereas the Athenian pottery has more stems and thin, drawn-out edges.

You might ask why I'm talking about pottery when I'm supposed to be writing you about families. That's because children, like clay, each have unique properties; there is a degree to which we can mold and shape them, but each of them have their own tensile strength. You have to work with the underline individual. You can't just stamp them out like a machine because what works with one kid could be a disaster with another.

There is a common adage that goes, "fair is not always equal, and equal is not always fair." If you've got kids or grandkids, I'm not telling you anything you don't already know. But we need to be reminded about these things because we feel so pressured sometimes as parents and grandparents to be "fair." We can sometimes find ourselves trying to treat them all exactly the same, when in reality, that's the most unfair thing you can do.

In my family, we have had two older kids and two younger ones over the course of more than twenty years. Naturally, a lot of things changed from the first set of kids to the second set. When the younger ones came along, my older son would sometimes say, "Hey, you didn't raise us like that."

One of my standard replies was, "Well, they aren't raising me the way you older kids did either."

You see, nobody knows how to be a parent

until they're a parent. Kids don't come into this world with a set of instructions stamped on their butts. I was learning as I went along the first time around, so of course there are bound to be differences with the other children. I would hope that I became wiser with experience.

A second standard reply was, "You're not your brother and you're not your sister, and I don't expect you to be a copy of them. If I treat you exactly like I treat your sister, it would be very unfair because that's not who you are."

As a father, I am supposed to learn who my children are and work with that. They should have the freedom to be true to themselves (within the boundaries of civilized society). It wouldn't be fair for me to try to make one child into a copy of the other.

So back to this idea of children and pottery. If you've never worked with clay, you should sometime just for the fun of it. When you're forming it in your hands or turning it on a wheel, you've got to use just the right kind of pressure, at just the right places, at just the right time. What happens to that lump of clay if you press too hard? It disintegrates or distorts which means you have to stop and put it all back into a lump. Once you pound it all down into a lump again, you have to start all over.

That's exactly what God does with His children, by the way. When life gets to the point where it presses in on us and makes us feel distorted or disintegrated, He stops the wheel, puts us back together, and starts reforming us. But He doesn't treat us all the same. Some of us will experience less distortion. Some of us will go through multiple reformations in our lifetime. Some of us will feel constant pressure.

And sometimes, we don't like that. We complain about why others seem to be blessed with more financial or familial success than us. But ultimately, we have to remember that God made us in His image and He never gives us more pressure than we can handle. The important thing is to remember that He is always working with us as we are because He sees what we can be. So, too, should we always be working to shape our children.

Development in Scripture

Abraham, his son Isaac and his grandson Jacob embody some of the dysfunctional family dynamics that have endured through time and hundreds of generations. In their stories, we find the typical arguing of brothers, and we can see how weaknesses found in the father often become the son's and grandson's weaknesses, too.

47

Recently, a puzzling question came up. "If Abraham was a liar, and his grandson Jacob was a con man, why did God choose them to be His chosen people?"

It's an interesting question. It's the same question you might ask about yourself as a modern Christian— "with all the mistakes I've made and all the stupid things I've done in my life, why would God even want me in His family?"

Or if we're more judgmental about it, we look at somebody else with our arms crossed and say, "why would God want them? What value could they possibly bring?"

God tells us why he chose Abraham. God said,

> "For I have chosen him, so that he will direct his children and his household after him to keep the way of the Lord by doing what is right and just, so that the Lord will bring about for Abraham what he has promised him" *(Genesis 18:19)*.

What's the point? God knew that Abraham was a guy that had lots of faults. There were things that Abraham did that were completely wrong. But it wasn't so much about what he had done before as it was about who he was inside and who he had the potential to become. It's as if God said, "I know he will teach his kids, and he'll teach them by doing what's right."

We can't just talk to our kids. We can't just tell them, "don't do what I do, do what I say."

If you choose to go that route, you will find that most kids will either rebel completely or end up following in your exact footsteps, only to stumble into the exact same pitfalls that you wanted them to avoid. Children and teenagers are always wrestling with the question of what is the right thing for them to do, and they are watching who you are as a person more than they are listening to what you say.

If you're a teacher, then you know they do the same thing to you when they're in the classroom. They listen to your words, and they watch what you do. They'll make the comparison and they'll quickly decide which rules you find important and which ones they can get away with breaking. If you say no cellphones in class, but you answer the phone during class time or text your friend about your plans for the weekend, then do you think those kids are going to take that rule seriously? Of course not.

Unfortunately, if kids have too many authority figures whose walk doesn't match the talk, they tend to become the ones that are lost to society, education and civilized culture. Why? Because people didn't tell them the right things? No. It's that the people they looked up to most didn't do the right things with their lives.

Does this mean that we have to be perfect in every way if we want our children to turn out halfway decently? Not at all. God chose Abraham, not because he was right about everything, but because he was good about most things.

Passing on Our Values to the Next Generation

A dispute arose among Jewish religious leaders in Jesus' day about which was the most important commandment in the Law of Moses. Out of the hundreds of laws, if you could only keep one, which should it be? Different rabbis would answer in different ways, and you could tell what "denomination" of Judaism you were with and which rabbi you followed by your belief on this topic *(Matthew 22:36-40)*.

So they came to Jesus and they asked him, "Which is the most important commandment?" Jesus answered that the most important law was "The Shema" found in *Deuteronomy 6:4-9*.

How did Moses originally teach that "most

important" law? Did he say, "Because you love the Lord your God make sure your doctrine is correct. Make sure once a week you go to the right building and sing the right song at the right time and say amen at the right place so that you may have all the appearances of a good Christian?" Is that what he said? No. The most important law of the Law of Moses was connected to the family.

What he said was, "these commandments that I give you today are to be on your hearts." Again we see this emphasis on having a good heart (as opposed to attaining perfection). Abraham did a lot of things wrong. There were things he believed that were not correct.

But remember why he was chosen by God? "For I have chosen him, so that he will direct his children and his household after him to keep the way of the Lord by doing what is right and just, so that the Lord will bring about for Abraham what he has promised him" *(Genesis 18:19)*. In other words, make sure YOU are well-grounded and worth being followed because your kids will more than likely do what you do and go where you lead them.

During weekday morning prayers, Orthodox and Conservative Jewish men wear Phylacteries, also called Tefillah, in an attempt to obey the teaching of *Deuteronomy 6:8*. Phylacteries are small, black, leather cubes containing a piece of parchment with *Exodus 13:1-16, Deuteronomy 6:4-9, or Deuteronomy 11:13–21* written on them. One is strapped to the left arm, and a second to the forehead. Some Jews who pray at the "Wailing" or "Western" Wall in Jerusalem can be seen wearing these.

Some Jewish houses today will actually have a little piece of metal that's attached to the door frame of the front door. It's called a mezuzah, and it's usually on the same side as the doorknob. If you look a little closer you can sometimes see something inside. What they've done is to actually take a little verse of scripture, put it inside this little metal thing, and placed it on the door frame *(Deuteronomy 6:9)*. When family members enter or exit, they see and touch it, reminding themselves that they are a family who try to honor God and His ways.

These aren't bad ideas if you are trying to instill a certain set of values into the next generation. But I think what God had in mind was something much deeper and more profound than merely external, impersonal displays on bodies and houses. God's word and God's ways need to be so deeply ingrained in your life that it can be seen when you walk, when you sit, when you eat, when you rise. It's not what you say, it's not something you do once a week, but rather, it's simply ingrained into the fabric of who and how you are. That's how the "authentic you" gets translated and transferred into the next generation.

One of the reasons I focus on teaching younger parents is because of what I hear so often from older parents whose kids are almost adults. Many older parents tell me things like, "I wish I had known in my 30's what I know today. I wish I had taken my kids to church. I wish I'd put them in touch with other Christian people. I wish we had said a prayer more at dinnertime. I wish I would've been home more, involved more and worked less." I've heard these things over and over. What are they saying? They're saying they wish they'd lived as *Deuteronomy 4:6-9* says we should.

Psalm 78 says that the most important truths are not new truths, they're old truths. And so while it's very important for our children to get an education in mathematics and science, it's even more important that they get an education in who God is and their role in the world. And how they can play into this grand scheme of the universe that's been going on for a long time. Those are things that are not taught with words, they're taught by actions.

"Raise up a child in the way he should go and when he's old he won't depart from it" *(Proverbs 22:6).* (I wrote about this in a previous chapter.) Remember, it's a proverb, not a promise. It's the way things generally work. You have to take into account the personality of kids and all these other kinds of circumstances.

But, generally speaking, we tend to return to the way we're reared. We tend to do what we were raised doing because that's what's comfortable and it's what we learned during our formative years. We return to those things because they are safe and familiar.

Here's something that isn't politically correct to say these days, but I'm going to say it anyway: God says that fathers have the ultimate responsibility for how families function. Fathers are responsible for their children's formation. Do mothers play a critical role? Naturally. But according to scripture, it's ultimately Dad's responsibility to see that his kids are formed correctly and that Mom isn't squeezing too loosely or too tightly. The problem is, you can't do that if your life is completely eaten up by things outside the home.

Too many men ignore or slight their leadership roles in their families, and too many women don't value and approve of that kind of position and authority for their children's father. But trust me— the older and more stubborn your kids are, the more they need a strong, loving, godly man of integrity in their lives! Regardless of your family's unique situation, it can only benefit your child to have a strong male role model in their life.

Guiding Questions: What Do Our Children Need to Know?

We mold our children through our actions. Every day, they look to us to figure out:

- What is most important?
- What's worth sacrificing for?
- What is success?
- What brings satisfaction?
- What's worthy of respect?
- How little can I do and still get by?
- What should I love and hate?
- What should I value?

The way our children answer these questions reveals a lot about their character. If that idea scares you, it shouldn't. There are many things you can do to help your child develop the integrity and values you want them to have.

5 Ways to Develop Your Child

Give Your Child Mentors

There's a certain age, usually about the time they become teenagers, when kids would rather chew off a leg than ask their parents for help or advice with tricky situations. It's at about this time that they begin to discover and form their own identities outside of the home. What our kids need during this process is mentors. In other words, we need to set them up with people that will tell them the exact same things we would tell them.

My family and I made a conscious effort to constantly put our kids around people that had our kind of values, morals, and mentalities. Sometimes it was coaches and teachers. Other times, it was other parents, aunts, uncles, or neighbors.

And, even though we understood what was happening, and even though we worked to make it happen, it still used to just drive me crazy when our kids valued the words and advice of others so highly. Sometimes they would quote one of these mentors saying something that was almost exactly what I had told them a week before. Events like those frustrated me, until it dawned on me that, regardless of the mechanism, they were listening and accepting the life-lessons I wanted them to get. And THAT'S what's really important in this, right? Not who gets credit, but who our children turn out to be.

Educate Your Child Morally

Another thing we've got to do to develop our children is to give them a moral education. Now, by "moral education," I mean learning how to apply timeless, ethical teachings to everyday life. We need to understand that kids are formed by the environment they're raised in. I believe we need to make sure that the environment we rear them in is as ethically and morally based as we possibly can make it. And we need to make it easier and more enjoyable to make the right decisions and to do the right things.

When I was a youth minister years ago, I'd sometimes have parents come to me saying, "I know my kids need a religious education, but I want them to make up their own mind, so I'm not gonna make 'em go to church."

Now, there's a point later on in life where that's true. But that point is not in the early to mid-formation days. What do you do with a child that's running a fever and says, "I don't wanna go to the doctor?" What do you do with a child that announces on Monday morning, "I don't wanna go to school." Do you tell them, "Okay, you make up your own mind. I don't want to warp your little psyche. I don't want to damage your self-esteem, so do what you want."?

Of course not. When they are older and more independent, then they can make their own decisions (and suffer their own consequences), but when they are still under your care, there are times they need to hear us tell them what's good for them and how they should act. Is it "harsh" to be the kind of parent that makes their children do what's right? Is it "mean" to hold our kids to high moral standards? I think it's essential.

Kids need a moral education if they are going to be successful in life. If we teach our kids how to be brilliant, but we don't teach them the ethics behind decisions, then what happens when they learn about something as powerful as nuclear energy? Nuclear energy can be a blessing or a curse, a bringer of energy or of destruction, depending on how it's used. Behind every scientific discovery, there is an ethical decision that needs to be made first.

Practice Hospitality

Practicing hospitality can include things like bringing people into our house, doing things for other people, and allowing other people to do things for us. When we interact with others through providing services, accepting help, and simply enjoying each other's company, we are modeling for our children what is important in life.

In a day and age where children would prefer communicating through texts or social media over face-to-face conversations, it's easy to see why some of our kids are growing up to be emotionally stunted and functionally immature. More than ever, teachers are having to teach our kids social-emotional skills that should be primarily taught in the home and merely reinforced in school.

But we can combat those issues through practicing hospitality and inviting people from all walks of life into our lives and the lives of our children. If they see us being gracious and kind, then they know what they should aspire to achieve. On the other hand, if they see us ignore our neighbors, avoid those who are different from us, or refuse to seek help (whether out of pride or stubbornness), then that is exactly what they will do in their own lives.

Set Realistic Expectations

Not every child is going to be another Einstein. When my wife was working on some classes for becoming a reading specialist, she told me about how different schools try to mask how a less-achieving student really is a less-achieving student. She said it could be a frustrating thing, because it IS important to be considerate about a student's feelings.

But at the core of the matter, it doesn't matter what you call them or what group you put them in. It's who they are, how they are, and what their individual abilities are. In her words at the time, "The Buzzard reading group doesn't change just because you call them Bluebirds." Some kids are simply never going to be educational geniuses.

Some kids have a knack for doing things with their hands. Some kids have a knack for creativity, mathematics, communication, or any number of areas. What matters isn't <u>what</u> our kids are good at, it's that we know our kids well enough to be able to see where their strengths and weaknesses are. We need to lovingly guide and encourage them in ways that will help them be successful in life. If their heart is set on being a doctor, but they're not any good at science and math, then we need to help them reevaluate their expectations and help them set goals that are a little more realistic.

This is an area where grandparents or mentors can be especially helpful. Sometimes what parents need is a little bit of separation from the idea that their kids must have this certain occupation or have to join this certain sport. If you are in a position to guide a child, then I believe you should help them discover occupations and life-goals that align well with their abilities and interests.

Make Them Work Hard

Generally speaking, families don't stress hard work as much as they used to. It used to be that one of the main ways to develop a child's character was through work. I'll bet that many of my readers would agree that their childhood was filled with physical labor of some sort.

I myself was raised this way. I used to wonder why my father always had a big garden in the summertime, until I realized that, since I worked there day after day, he knew exactly where I was even when school was out.

A lot of who I am today came about as a result of working in Dad's garden -- learning how to cultivate potatoes, how to cut the weeds out and leave the good plants, etc. When you grow rhubarb, which part of the plant is good to eat (the stems) and which part isn't? (the leaves.) What happens to the potatoes if you don't cultivate them? (The exposed potato skin gets little green tinge on them.)

I learned an awful lot about plants, but I learned more about me than I did about gardening. Ironically, to this day, I hate gardening. I'd rather you raise the stuff and let me buy it from you. We don't have a yearly garden today. However, I don't resent my father for making me do it because it was an invaluable teaching tool.

The value was not in that I suddenly became a world-class gardener. I value it because of the things I gained: a good work ethic, experience working with tools, time management, and creative thinking. I learned little things like— if you take a little time in the beginning to sharpen your hoe, then you'll do twice as much work twice as fast. Or, you can forget about sharpening it, jump right in, and it'll take you two or three times longer. Today, the tools I usually use are books, calendars, phones and a computer, but I still use all of the things that I learned in those sweltering summer days.

Hard work teaches kids about the millions of small details that go into forming a productive, successful life for themselves. But if kids aren't ever given jobs (whether around the house or in a family business), if they're not expected to work diligently or put forth effort, then they are missing out on a crucial medium of character formation. Many families make the excuse that, "I don't want my kids to have to work like I did." Or, I've also heard many a mom say, "it's easier for me to just wash the dishes than to get her to do it."

Time out. We're not washing dishes, we're raising kids. Oh, to be sure, there will be arguments and headaches and days when you just want to throw up your hands in defeat. But if you continuously set the expectation for your kids that they must contribute in whatever way they physically can, then you will be setting them up for success.

Closing Thoughts

Shaping a child is less about what you say and more about what you do. The way you "work the clay" is by living the way you would want them to live. Your kids watch what you spend your time doing and what you spend your money on. They watch what you push them to excel in and what you let them slide on. They notice what's important to you and what's not important to you. They see past your words and into the heart of who you are as a person, not just what you try to be as a parent.

All of the actions you take in your day-to-day life are like little pressure points on this lump of clay. If you've got more than one kid, then you're working on multiple lumps of clay at the same time, and the different pieces of clay respond differently to the same level of pressure. So with one lump of clay you've got to be a little more firm, while with the other, you've got to be a little lighter. It's not easy, and it does require a bit of creativity at times, but through all this, they're watching and they're trying to answer basic questions about life.

I read a quote not too long ago that said, "Children seldom do what their parents say, but they almost always wind up doing what their parents do." How many of you grew up saying, "I'll never be like my parents" or "I'll never say that to my children!" only to find yourself, 20 years later, repeating one of your parent's expressions or subconsciously picking up a habit of theirs?

Even if you are determined to do the exact opposite of what they did, that still goes to show how deeply we are affected by the actions of our parents. We are the first example for our children of how to behave and what to value. We need to live our lives as we would want our children to live theirs.

So, I want to ask you this question: what are you <u>doing</u> to form your children and grandchildren well? To be clear, lecturing them or quoting scripture does not count. I'm not asking you if you <u>told</u> them how to be good people. I'm asking, *if they lived the rest of their life as you are living yours, would they be okay?*

If they adopt your attitude toward any mundane topic— paying taxes, working, being a Christian, obeying traffic laws, etc.— would they be wholesome people? If you can't give me an unequivocal yes, then you have a problem. Remember, sometimes who we are shouts so loudly that people can't hear what we're saying.

We can say that God is what's most important to us, but if we spend more money on our car than we give to God, then our kids begin to internalize that giving to God is not as important as having nice things. Kids learn by <u>formation</u> rather than <u>information</u>. The environment that we produce for them and the priorities we set for ourselves all help cast the mold or pattern for our children to model themselves after. And once that clay is set and dried, it becomes almost impossible to recast.

The good news is that today is your chance to make a new start. You could make things right with God and with other people. You could start showing your children and grandchildren a higher level of concern for His things and His ways. You could start setting the right example in the area of how you treat other people. It's never too late to know God's love and live as He would want you to live. The rest will take care of itself.

Prayer

Oh God, we live in a broken and fallen world. We see all around us the results in our schools, our government, our neighborhoods and our families. We see the results of people not doing things your way. Father, we're sorry. We're saddened that children have to pay the price for our neglect and for us not living as we should.

We pray, Father, that you would give us healing and mercy. We pray that you would bring people and events into our children and grandchildren's lives that would fill the holes that we leave.

And we ask, God, that you would heal us from the inside, so that if our children and grandchildren copy our hearts and our actions, they'll be well on the path to success in their own lives. In Christ's name we pray. Amen.

ROCKS FOR FAMILIES

"Discipline literally means training that is expected to produce a specific character or pattern of behavior.

Discipline is not just punishment, and it is not just a method for bringing a parent peace of mind.

Good discipline shapes and molds children for their good.

It helps me to view discipline as setting limits and enforcing some form of consequence for breaking those limits."

-7 Habits of a Healthy Home by *Bill Carmichael*

Rock 3: Fences — What Are the Rules?

When it comes to parenting, we don't have to agree about everything in order to be friends. How (and if) we discipline our children is one of the biggest areas of contention, but make no mistake, it is one of the most critical.

We've all known a child that had no concept of boundaries. They are the ones who go running up and down the aisles in grocery stores, airplanes, and churches. They scream when they should be whispering, they interrupt when they should wait patiently, they ignore adults when they should be saying "yes ma'am" or "yes sir." And through it all, you'll see the parents looking exhausted, fed up, and embarrassed. Or, you'll see a parent overreact and start fussing and hollering over a situation they should have never allowed to get that far.

But it doesn't have to be like this. If we are proactive in setting up "fences" or boundaries for our children, then we will hardly ever have to be reactive. Punishment alone is not discipline. If we want to instill discipline in our children, then we need to begin by explicitly showing our children what acceptable behavior looks like.

When our children were very young, we knew an older mother who spanked her kids with a wooden spoon. And she'd say, "I promise, this will hurt **you** more than **me** because you earned it and you're going to get it." She seemed to use the discipline of her children as a vent for her own anger. That's not true discipline. The only thing those kids learned from her is how to be angry and how to use physical aggression to make yourself feel better.

Then, when I was older, I found that there were some parents who seemed to go too far in the opposite direction. For whatever reason (exhaustion, lack of caring, or not wanting to "stifle" their children), they didn't discipline their children at all, not even for their children's own good. Those children learned that they could do whatever they want and there would be no consequences.

Maybe you heard the story of the teenager from Texas who received probation for killing 4 people while driving drunk. His defense? He claimed that his whole life, nobody ever told him no, and that's why he didn't know any better than to get in the car while drunk. Now, that's obviously no excuse for drunk driving. But imagine what kind of a person he could have been had his parents not indulged him at every turn? Would those people still be alive if his parents had actually put forth the effort or caring to show him right from wrong? We may never know for sure. The bottom line, however, is discipline shouldn't be avoided simply because it's difficult to follow through on. The consequences could be disastrous.

We should have two purposes for disciplining our children: to ensure their immediate welfare (that is, making sure they're not doing anything to hurt themselves or others) and to guide their future (in other words, we instill in them the values they need to be successful). It shouldn't be about the adults at all. But our world today often gets that backwards. Money, politics, and the desires of the adults in charge seem to drive the decision-making processes that directly impact our children. It's sad, and it's our kids that suffer.

Raising disciplined children and punishing children are not the same thing. When you have to discipline your child for breaking a rule, it's not about you being on a power trip over controlling your child. That's just punishment for the sake of punishment. If you hurt your child out of frustration or to make yourself feel better, that sets a dangerous precedent and doesn't teach that child anything about being a better adult.

Discipline, on the other hand, is about building metaphorical fences— setting limits or defining unacceptable behaviors for your child— and enforcing some form of consequence for crossing that line. You don't have to get angry to do that. You don't have to be upset. You shouldn't discipline your children or grandchildren after they've pushed your last nerve and now you blow up like Vesuvius. True discipline requires you to be upfront with your expectations, to clearly communicate the consequences of not meeting those expectations, and to follow through when they inevitably hop the proverbial fence.

6 "Fences" for Instilling Discipline

Set Godly Expectations... And Then Follow Them

Just as I said in the previous chapter, we should be a living testament to the kind of life we want our children to live. Most of us have had a manager who loved to send out memos or dictate in extreme detail the things that employees cannot do, and then they proceeded to break every one of the rules they claimed were so important. Did you enjoy following every single one of those rules? Probably not (if you followed any of them at all).

So, be genuine with your children. Live a godly life and set godly expectations that are age-appropriate. If you hold yourself to similar standards, then they will have no excuses for not following them and be less likely to resent the limits that you set for them.

When You Say "NO," Mean It

I believe that, when dealing with our kids, we should say "yes" about everything that we possibly can. Why? Because that's the way God, our Father is. When you go to your Father in heaven and ask Him for something, the only time He tells you no is because it's wrong for you or society, or it's not good for you right now.

I used to think that God decided to make everything fun a sin. I finally figured out that sins are the things that are fun short-term but that will make your life miserable in the long run.

For example, one reason you don't sleep with another person's spouse is because it's a good way to wind up dead, right? You can look at the situation in one of two ways: from the betrayed spouse's point of view or the adulterer's point of view. Murder might make the betrayed party feel better in the moment, but then they have to deal with emotional trauma, physical incarceration, and a criminal record ruining their future. Conversely, intercourse might make someone feel physical pleasure in the moment, but they can suffer physical illness, retaliation, a messy divorce/breakup, and loss of reputation.

The point is, God tells us yes about everything He possibly can, so we as parents and grandparents ought to do the same. When we say no, it should be because it's in our child's best long-term interest. For many parents, their first answer is automatically no. Then the kids keep pestering them over and over and over until their no becomes yes. So what did the child learn from that interaction? That your no isn't absolute. So, in their minds, it stands to reason that those rules you set for them might not be as important as you said either. And that's exactly what Jesus said not to do. Jesus said, "Let your yes be yes and your no be no" *(Matthew 5:37)*.

When you say yes, you should seriously mean yes. I adopted this with my kids when they were very young. My kids learned that, not only could they get me to say yes pretty easily, they also learned that if I told them they could do something, I'd move heaven and earth to make it happen for them. But what they also understood was that, when I did on rare occasion say no, it was because it must be something I'm serious about. That's how I helped them internalize the discipline that I wanted them to have.

Less is More

I'll use my wife and her students as an example. If she gave her students a list of 20 rules on the board at the beginning of the year, but she was really only committed to enforcing 6 of those rules, then why would those children follow any of her rules? Not only that, but what child can honestly remember that many specific rules? She would spend half her time and energy trying to get children to behave. Far better to have a few major expectations that were general enough to cover a variety of situations. "Be responsible" is a heck of a lot easier to say and remember than: "turn in your homework on time," "show up with a pencil and paper every day, "work hard in group projects," and "follow the teacher's instructions." See the difference?

In your family, be wise in choosing where to stand firm. Anchor your non-negotiables in virtues and values, not in whims and personal preferences. Once you have decided what is most important to you, make five or six major rules that are general enough to cover a variety of situations. Also, take the time to explain your rules instead of letting kids learn by trial and error what you do or do not expect of them. You can't have piles and piles of rules that you never explained (or in some parent's cases, have never enforced), and then get angry and punish them when they end up crossing the line they didn't even remember existed. You've got to teach them your expectations and then <u>be consistent.</u>

Explain Expectations Clearly

When you are entering into a new situation, you need to make it absolutely clear what you expect your children to say and how you expect them to act. How many times have you told your children that they better "act right?" Now, how many times have you actually explained to them what "acting right" looks like?

Let's say you're taking your toddler to the grocery store, and this is the first time that you are going to let them walk around instead of sitting in the cart. You probably shouldn't just waltz in without talking to your child, unless you just enjoy chasing after a wandering three year old before they shout rude things at the top of their lungs and knock over a display they had no business touching in the first place.

Instead, you should have a chat with them before you even take them out of their car seat. Explain to them what things should and should not look like as they walk through the store. For example, you might say to them, "you will walk next to the cart the whole time, you will use your inside voice, and you will not touch anything." Once you've gone to the store a couple times and your child has met those expectations, then there's no need to continuously bring it up because they have internalized that expectation. It might take a little more effort in the beginning, but it will save you so much trouble in the long run.

Let Them Reap What They Sow

If you have done your job well (outlined expectations of behavior, explained the rules, explained the consequences, etc.), and your children still cross the line, then they must suffer the consequences of their own actions. As a youth minister, I used to find that there were times when kids would make mistakes or do something wrong. Yet, when we would show the parents the proof or bring a witness, they refused to believe that their children were capable of doing wrong. Or they made excuse after excuse as to why their child had done it. Unbelievable.

Now look, I know the truth about my kids. They are generally good kids that make good decisions. There are some choices that would be out of character for them to make, but, given the right (or wrong) circumstances, there's nothing that my kids "wouldn't do." There's always the possibility that they make a dumb decision or say something hurtful, but you don't handle those kinds of problems by ignoring or denying them. You handle them by letting them suffer the consequences of whatever their choices are. If a kid wrecks the car, you don't just automatically give them a new car. Maybe you take away their driving privileges or their cell phone. Maybe you find a way for them to earn the money you spent on the deductible. Maybe you buy them a crummy replacement until they show they are responsible enough to own a nicer car again.

Will they be upset or embarrassed about having to walk, not having a cell phone, not being able to hang with their friends, or having to drive a shabby car? Maybe. I hope so. The more it "hurts" the faster they'll learn the life-lesson. If they can learn some things about responsibility, safety, and taking care of their things, for the price of a little sweat and embarrassment, then I think it's a cheap lesson. Learning those same things in front of a judge with a gavel or trying to outrun a cop with a gun would be MUCH more costly!

I know we want our children to be happy, but if you always shield your children from consequences or hardship, if you are constantly making excuses for them or turning a blind eye to their faults, then you are doing them a disservice. You are trading their minor discomfort now for major character flaws in the future. Ask yourself what kind of person they will be when they have left your home or when you have left this earth. If you're unhappy with the answers you find, then you know what you need to do.

Letting Go

There is this idea in education called "gradual release." Now, what it means in the classroom is that the teacher will model for the students how something is done, do the activity together as a class, let them try it in groups, and finally let them try the activity independently. Your home is not a classroom (obviously there isn't as much group work or homework involved), but there is a lot to be said for gradually shifting and releasing responsibility for your children's behavior from you to them.

Think back to the grocery store example. I said that, the very first time, you would have to explicitly walk your child through everything that you expected them to do and not do. Would you still have that talk with your 30-year-old child? Of course not! You could, but you would get a lot of strange looks. That's because, <u>after a while, your kids get it.</u> They know how they should behave, and if they don't, then that's on them to suffer the consequences. So ideally, you go over your expectations the first few trips. Then, you start going straight into the store, and you review the expectations as needed when they start acting up. Eventually, you don't have to say anything to them, and they consistently behave the way they should without a word from you. Ultimately, they can go to the store by themselves and neither one of you have to think twice about it.

I know it's a simplistic example, but it applies to everything we try to teach them about as they are growing up. We love our children, and we love to feel needed by them, but we can't let ourselves cling to this idea that they should be babied forever. The sad reality is, we will not always be there for them. Now, I don't know about you, but I want to die knowing that my children will be able to be good people even if I'm no longer on this earth. If you don't get them to internalize your expectations, if they don't "buy-in" to the values that you have set forth for your family, then they will not continue to follow your lessons the way that you want them to.

That is why punishment and fear will never be as effective as discipline and clear-cut expectations. If your child fears you, they will listen to you as long as you are around. If your child respects you, then they will take your lessons to heart long after they move away to live their own lives.

Boundaries and Responsibilities in Scripture

Parents and Children Have Different Responsibilities

We can learn a lot about Boundaries and Responsibility from scripture. *Ezekiel 18:4* says, "Everyone belongs to me, the parent, as well as the child, both alike belong to me." The last sentence of that verse says, "The one who sins is the one who will die."

You might ask how that is relevant to parenting. The principle is that, while we are all responsible **to** each other, we are not responsible **for** each other.

Think carefully about this.

Imagine a girl coming into a math class and saying, "I'm not any good at math because my dad's bad at math and I've got bad math genes." Does that hold water? No. Because the one who fails the math test is the one that fails the math test. See? The one that sins, is the one that dies. That's how God views things like this. We can have the best parents in the world and still sin. We can have the worst parents in the world and still be compassionate.

To be clear, I'm not saying that a grandparent or parent's job doesn't matter at all. It's a parent's responsibility to make sure they have set up systems of discipline and taught their children high expectations for life. But at some point, it becomes the child's responsibility to do what is expected of them. We can help them deal with the consequences of their actions, but if they knew better, then it is not your place to blame yourself or make excuses for them.

I love my children. I pray for my children. I did everything I could to give them the best family possible. But you know, I've made lots of mistakes along the way. There were times I was a horrible father, but I was always trying to give them my best. And, God willing, they'll do better than me.

But now that they're grown, they're the one that has to pick a lane on the highway of their own lives. Whatever path they choose, if your kids don't like where their road in life is headed, they can only blame themselves for picking that fork in the road. You do your best as parents to set them on the right path, but at some point they have to move forward without you. All you can do is hope that you have programmed their "GPS" well enough that they don't stray too far from their destination.

Our Responsibilities to Society

"The word of the Lord came to me, son of man, speak to your people and say to them, 'When I bring the sword against a land and the people of the land choose one of their men to make him their watchman, and he sees the sword coming against the land and blows the trumpet to warn the people, then if anyone hears the trumpet but does not heed the warning, when the sword comes and takes their life, their blood will be on their own head. If they had heeded the warning, they would've saved themselves. But if the watchman sees the sword coming and does not blow the trumpet to warn the people and the sword comes and takes someone's life, that person's life will be taken because of their sin, but I will hold the watchman accountable for their blood.'"

In our families, parents and grandparents can see some things in life very clearly; we've earned this clarity through our choices, the mistakes we've made, and the things that have happened to us in life. And there are times that we can look and see that one of our children or grandchildren is not in a good place or that they're headed in a wrong direction. And in that case, we have become a "watchman," and we need to warn them about the future trouble that lies ahead. It doesn't matter whether that other person is your grandchild, your own child, a friend of your child, a neighbor's kid, or somebody you work with. You have a responsibility as the wiser person to at least offer your perspective.

The Bible is very clear about the fact that, as a society, we are all in this together, but that the ultimate responsibility falls to the individual. In other words, we are not responsible **for** each other, just **to** each other. If you see someone younger or less experienced than you struggling, and you don't intercede, then you will be "accountable for their blood." If they choose to ignore your experiences and repeat your mistakes, then "their blood will be on their own head." When it comes to your children, you've got to do what you've got to do to get that child on the right path. But once you've done what you can, it's out of your control.

And that's where the disagreement can be, right? Kids sometimes think that it's their parents' fault and parents think it's somebody else's responsibility to fix the parent's or child's mistakes. I've forgotten the number of times as a youth minister that parents would come to me in tears saying that their minor child (who hadn't been to church in several years) is rebelling or getting into trouble with the law and asking me if was there anything I could do to fix them.

Our teachers struggle with similar things in school. No one can undo with a few hours in a classroom what happens the rest of the day at home. Yet, people are constantly asking teachers to compensate for a lifetime of mis-teachings in the home. That's not right. Teachers should do what they can, of course, but at some point, it's out of their hands.

Our Actions Bring Reactions

In *Matthew 10:11-15*, Jesus talks about how our actions bring reactions. Jesus sends his disciples out on a mission trip, and he says,

> "whatever town or village you enter, search there for some worthy person and stay at

their house until you leave. As you enter the home, give it your greeting. If the home is deserving, let your peace rest on it. If not, let your peace return to you. If anyone will not welcome you or listen to your words, leave that home or town and shake the dust off your feet. Truly I tell you, it will be more bearable for Sodom and Gomorrah on the Day of Judgment than for that town."

Once again, there is a clear-cut division of responsibility. The disciples had the responsibility to go out and be his messengers, but Jesus acknowledges that whether their message was successfully received or not is not within their control. Their responsibility was only to convey the message to the best of their abilities. The rest lies in the hands, heads, and hearts of the ones that are being taught. That's just as relevant today with our kids and grandkids.

As people in authority over the next generation, we've got to try everything we can to the best of our abilities. We can't just sit back and say that it's not our responsibility or that we are afraid to tell them when they are doing wrong things. The point is we've got to give each one of them our best. If they choose a different way to live or they choose to ignore your teachings, then you've done all that you can do. It's in God's hands after that.

If you have more than one child, it's easy to fall into complacency and carelessness. When you had the first one, you were probably overly worried, and you laser-focused on them. You were trying to get everything just-right. But with each subsequent child, it gets easier to relax, ease up and let more things slide. Most of us have seen or heard some version of the joke about the baby dropping the pacifier. With the first baby, the pacifier goes into a bag and gets boiled. With the second baby, it gets taken to a sink and rinsed off. With the third baby, it gets wiped off on your jeans. And with the fourth, you just give it back to them. As parents, we can laugh about that.

But what if we slack off with things that are really important (honesty, work ethic, relationship to God, and service to other people)? By the time we're with the second, third or fourth child, grandchildren or great grandchildren, we sometimes make the mistake of thinking that our work is done or that we are too tired to help someone learn these lessons all over again.

Society can't afford for that to happen. Your family cannot afford for that to happen. If you're still alive, and you're still breathing, your kids and grandkids still need you. Give them your best, and whatever reactions they have is for them to deal with.

Self-control vs. Parent-control

"Make a tree good and its fruit will be good or make a tree bad and its fruit will be bad, for a tree is recognized by its fruit. You brood of vipers, how can you who are evil say anything good? For the mouth speaks what the heart is full of. A good man brings things out of the good stored in him and an evil man brings evil things out of the evil stored in him."

-Matthew 12:33-35

I wanted to look at this passage to reiterate that our reasons for our actions come from deep within, not imposed from without. In other words, our goal as parents and grandparents should not be to run our kids' lives for them. Our goal should be to teach them to run their own lives well. Do you see the difference? As a child-rearer, it takes completely different skill sets to micromanage a child versus teaching them self-management. Remember when I said that there was a huge difference between a child fearing you and a child respecting you? Or between merely punishing a child physically and instilling discipline? This is a similar concept.

It's easy enough to control their every move

when they are younger. A toddler or infant depends on you for everything and has relatively few avenues of rebellion. Oh sure, your toddler can kick and scream, but eventually, you can get them to do exactly what you want. You can tell them what's for dinner, what they're going to wear, when they'll get to see their friends, what sports to do — the possibilities are endless. But as they get older, your children and grandchildren find ways to get away from you and your influence. They start ripping the apron strings out of your hands.

Sooner or later, their true self is going to come out. That's why we've got to help them be good people inside, not just puppets who know how to make themselves look good to the outside world when we are watching them. What happens when we aren't there to watch? What kind of "tree" will they reveal themselves to be? What kind of "fruit" will they bear?

The father that raised Joseph also raised some boys who were ready to kill their brother *(Genesis 37).* Granted, there was some unwise parental favoritism, but even so, what was the difference? Why did one boy turn out so kind and sweet, yet the others so envious and ruthless? They were not good people. Hopefully, Joseph's father did his best, but there the responsibility ended.

When Israel needed a king to replace Saul, the prophet Samuel was sent to a house with several brothers *(1 Samuel 16).* He met all the sons, and none of them seemed to be the one.

The prophet asked the father, "is there not another brother?"

"There is still the youngest," Jesse answered. "He is tending the sheep."

The family was dismissive of David's value, but when Samuel was considering one of the other brothers, the Lord said to Samuel, "Do not consider his appearance or his height, for I have rejected him. The Lord does not look at the things people look at. People look at the outward appearance, but the Lord looks at the heart" *(1 Samuel 16:7).*

Acts 13:22 says, "After removing Saul, he made David their king. God testified concerning him: 'I have found David son of Jesse, a man after my own heart; he will do everything I want him to do.'"

The thing that makes the greatest long-term difference in how a life turns out has always been, and always will be the inner qualities of the heart, not the outer actions of the hands. So keep that in mind as you raise your children. Remember that you want them to understand what is right and wrong, not simply to follow orders. Help them discover the goodness and godliness that resides in their heart.

Discipline Verses in Scripture

- Getting obedience and respect from children takes effort and enforcement *(1 Timothy 3:4-5).*
- Parents should deal with their children the way God deals with them *(Hebrews 12:5-11).*
- Punishment is sometimes required to mold a child's character *(Proverbs 13:24; 22:15; 23:13; 29:15-17).*

I believe that parents should deal with their children the way God deals with them. Getting obedience and respect from children takes enforcement and effort. You can't just tell them, "Don't do that. Don't do that, don't do that. Don't do that. I'm going to get you. I'm going to do it. I'm gonna spank you. Don't do it. Wait till your father hears about this." Have you ever witnessed something like this in a restaurant or in an aisle at Wal-Mart?

That's not anywhere close to effective, and

it's not how God would treat us. Tell them once, and then let them face the consequences. If your child is misbehaving in the grocery store, tell them, "if you don't act right in this check-out line, you're not getting that candy bar." And if they keep not acting right, what should you do? Let them have the candy so they don't scream and embarrass you? No! You take away the candy bar and you let them scream and embarrass you. Why? Because it's not about you. It's about them.

My mom once told the story about when I was little. I wanted something in the store and she wouldn't get it for me. She said that I had learned from some other kids at a babysitter's house that if you threw a temper tantrum, you could get what you wanted. She said that I plopped down on the store's floor and kicked and screamed, and instead of giving in or ignoring me, she just sat down on the floor and kicked and screamed too.

I don't remember any of this, but supposedly I said something along the lines of, "Mom, people are looking at you." And she responded with, "well, people are looking at you too. Get up." I didn't get the candy bar, but I stopped making a fool of myself. As parents, we've got to be willing to face some embarrassment and some hardship for the good of our kids and grandkids. But if that fails, if a child continues to act disrespectfully or in a manner that endangers someone, then you need to move on to more serious consequences.

To Spank or Not

Here's where I'll say something that you might disagree with. *This is my opinion. It's a biblically based opinion, but it's my opinion and you have the right to disagree.* I think spanking should be used, but only as a last resort, not a first resort.

Sometimes the only way to mold a child's character is through reasonable physical punishment. Now, as I said earlier when I was talking about discipline, anger should play no part in it. After all, there's a huge difference among discipline, punishment, and child abuse. We're talking about spanking a child, not beating them, neglecting them, or leaving a lasting or damaging mark. It's most people's least favorite part of parenting, but I believe it is sometimes a necessary one.

I remember my great granddad was a carpenter. He used to wear this old green cap that had a button on the top. I used to help him on small construction projects. I can remember two or three times that he told me to do something and I didn't obey him. He'd usually tell me a second time. But if he had to tell me a third time, the cap came off and the button popped me on top of the head. I didn't need stitches. I didn't have any broken bones. But I learned quickly that when Daddy Sam said to do something, he meant for me to hop up quickly and go do it. Did it hurt? Very briefly. Did it damage me emotionally? I don't think so. I like to think that I'm a better man today because he used a cap button to get my attention and refocus me.

If your child has ignored their chances, don't hesitate to spank them. I can count on one hand the number of times I've swatted my kids more than just a pat. But I can guarantee that each one of those kids remembers it, and they didn't want it again. Why? Because "yes" is so much more fun than "no," and they quickly learned that when you push too far, you're not going to get what you want to get.

There's a passage in the Bible that really speaks to me about the ultimate purpose of discipline. In *Hebrews 12:9-11*, it says,

> "we have all had human fathers who disciplined us and we respected them for it.... They disciplined us for a little while as they thought best; but God disciplines us for our good, in order that we may share in his

holiness. No discipline seems pleasant at the time, but painful. Later on, however, it produces a harvest of righteousness and peace for those who have been trained by it."

The words "harvest of righteousness" really stand out to me. The true spirit of discipline is that your children become adults that know the difference between right and wrong in their own hearts.

So, if you are helping raise a child, do whatever you need to do to give them the very best shot at a successful life. Do it lovingly, but do it. We parents, grandparents, aunts, and uncles need to be the ones to teach the next generation how to survive in this society that we've built. If we turn them loose before they're ready, if we just let them go their own way and do what they want to do, we shouldn't be surprised if society starts to break down. The solution is in our own hands, and that's the way God intended it.

Consider This

- Spanking should be used as a last resort, not a first resort -- give yourself time to think.
- Speak calmly to your child before the spanking. Explain why they are being

punished.
- Give only as many swats as are needed to make your point.
- Hug your child when you are finished and reassure them of your love.
- Don't hesitate to do it if it's needed!

Prayer

God, we ask that you fill our children's hearts with kindness and strength. Open their minds to your teachings and those of their parents, Lord. Help the parents and grandparents of the world find the courage to set godly expectations for themselves and their children.

Father, we know that our children will one day leave us, but help us prepare them for the cruel realities of the world around them. Through you, Lord, we know that all things are possible. May they grow strong enough to make the world a gentler and better place. In Jesus's name, amen.

ROCKS FOR FAMILIES

"Happiness cannot be traveled to, owned, earned, worn or consumed.

Happiness is the spiritual experience of living every minute with love, grace, and gratitude."

-Denis Waitley

Rock 4: Rejoicing — Am I Important? Is Life Good?

Festivity. Jubilation. Celebration. The best families, regardless of their size or situation, practice all of these in abundance. One of the most significant indicators of a child's future success is their capacity to show joy and gratitude.

Let me tell you a story about a grandfather that had two grandsons whose personalities were as different as night and day. One grandson was a very gloomy and negative child. He always seemed to find something to complain about or be worried about. The other grandson had a positive and upbeat attitude no matter what the circumstances.

One day, the grandfather took the gloomy grandson to a big huge barn filled with wrapped packages. When the grandfather told him they were all for him, the boy sat down and started crying. He complained that his parents were always telling him to make his room clean, and now he would have to find a place to put all of these things away. He was so busy thinking about all the stress and work these presents would cause that he forgot all about being thankful he received them in the first place!

Next, the grandfather took the other grandson to a different barn filled nearly to the rafters with horse manure in every stall. Now, most people would be disgusted or upset, but the kid jumped in squealing and laughing and digging around. When the grandfather asked why he was so happy, he said that with all this horse stuff, there's gotta be a pony in here somewhere! Here is a kid in what looks like a terrible situation, but he still maintains a bright, sunny disposition. He still has hope. That's what we've got to cultivate in the hearts of our children. They need to develop the ability to have "hope in the middle of despair," instead of "despair in the middle of hope."

Where do our children learn to rejoice in the little things and count their blessings not their hardships? That's right, they learn it at home. If their parents and grandparents are constantly anxious about the future or upset because of this, that or the other, then how is that child supposed to maintain a positive outlook on life? You can see why it is crucial to deliberately celebrate the good in our lives.

Something that my wife and I have done as a couple ever since we were first dating is go out and enjoy live music. It never mattered if it was just a little hole in the wall place with a guy strumming a guitar on a raggedy stool or if it was a huge arena with stadium lights and chanting crowds. We just loved going to these kind of things.

I remember one Winterfest concert we went to several years ago. We usually sent the kids each winter, and one year, when we went ourselves, the Newsboys performed. One of their songs was something about life being good, and everything coming down with confetti and roses and rainbows. After that song, they had an encore. There was a loud boom, and from overhead, all this confetti dropped, like a metallic rain. When the lights hit it, everything sparkled and shined, and this sense of elation just ran through everyone like a zap of electricity. It was a magical moment to be a part of. Sadly, there are some people who go their whole lives without allowing themselves to feel that kind of joy.

Rejoicing All Life

All Things Work for Good

When the angel came to the shepherds to announce the birth of Jesus, the angelic message was a celebration of life, "I bring you good news that will cause great joy for all the people" *(Luke 2:10-12)*. I'm always sad when I hear parents say things like, "well you know we really didn't want to have any kids, but she got pregnant and..." If you phrase it that way, what does it communicate to that child?

If a child feels unwanted or like a burden, then you are polluting the soil they are growing in. It is unbelievably hard to overcome that kind of emotional trauma. That's why I am very conscientious of how I tell the story about how my wife found out she was pregnant with our daughter. We could easily talk about how I had just lost my job, we were on the tail end of a business bankruptcy, and my marriage was being torn apart at the seams due to the stress of it all. But in reality, having her brought me back to my family and saved my marriage. It is because of her that I've been a full-time minister for nearly 30 years. Her birth <u>literally</u> changed the trajectory of my life. If I'd stayed on the path I was on, I would have strayed from my duties as a family man. For all outward appearances, I was still a good guy. I still went to and helped with the church. But inside the privacy of my home, my heart just wasn't in it anymore. I was so focused on the negatives that I allowed the storm to blow me off course; her birth put me on the path back to my family. Now that's something to celebrate!

Just like the two boys with their grandfather,

how you frame the story is how you frame your life. Successful families frame their stories in positive, celebratory ways. As Christians, we know that "in all things, God works for the good of those who love him, who have been called according to his purpose" *(Romans 8:28)*. But you can't just <u>say</u> it; you have to <u>live</u> it. If you believe that it's true in church, but you act differently at home, then your children will pick up on that. When you're in the middle of the storm, it's your job to figure out the good thing that God is trying to do with it. Show your children that, through faith and perseverance, there will always be something to celebrate in the end. It might not turn out the way that you had originally planned, but you've got to believe that there is more to it than despair. All things won't <u>be</u> good, but all things will work <u>for</u> good.

Purpose and Blessings

In *Genesis 5:28-29*, after Lamech had lived 182 years, he had a son who he named Noah. Lamech named him Noah and said, "he will comfort us in the labor and painful toil of our hands caused by the ground the Lord has cursed." Many times throughout the Old Testament, the father would lay his hands on the child and bless them in a way that foretold their personality and what their destiny in life would be. A similar thing happened with Jacob and his 12 sons as he lay on his deathbed. His dying words prophesied their destinies, and each one eventually came to fruition, whether good or bad *(Genesis 49:1-27)*.

The point is, every child has a purpose, and every child has a way that it can bless our families, our communities, and our future. Every child. I don't need to know your child to know that they are a blessing; I know the God who made your child. Just because you might have had or are having problems with your children, doesn't mean that they weren't put on this earth for a reason.

Our country has failed its children horribly. Abortions will one day be a dark stain on the history of this nation. In the future, when they look back on the decades of the abortions that our country has condoned, abortion will be seen as an atrocity on level with the Holocaust in Germany, the Pol Pot regime in Southeast Asia, or Caligula's reign in Rome. Why? Because, as a country, we don't believe that every child has a meaning and a purpose. If they aren't wanted, convenient, or perfectly timed, then they aren't useful or something to celebrate? That's simply not true.

Love in Action

We should celebrate every child with joy, no matter what the circumstances behind their conception. When our kids think about their place in our family, what do they think and feel? You might love them wholeheartedly and think they are a special blessing from God, but do they know that? It might sound cheesy, but how often do you communicate your feelings to them? Do your actions reflect how you feel about them? Do you act like they are a joy to you? When they invite you to go to one of their games or performances, are you eager to go? Or is the hesitation and dismay written all over your face?

My wife and I personally think soccer is terribly boring. We don't even enjoy watching professional games, much less a group of kids who aren't that talented. And don't get me started on the weather. They play soccer whether it's raining or the temperatures are down in the 40s, but at least they're running around staying a little bit warm. What are Dad, Mom, Grandpa, and Grandma doing? Freezing our hands and ears while sitting on a hard bench (if they even have benches). And yet, if my kids or grandkids wanted me there, then you can bet that we would be there. And when they ask us if we're gonna be at the next one, I'm gonna say "of course!" Because when they become adults and they look back on those games, they probably won't remember the score or their personal performance. They'll remember that their family loved and supported them no matter what. That's so important.

If our interactions with children aren't colored with joy, if we're constantly complaining and picking at them for one insignificant thing or another, then when they think about us, they won't think of us as a force of love. They'll think about how nothing is ever good enough. They'll grow up believing that your love has stipulations, limitations, and dissatisfaction.

Kids will always mess up. Even adults, as God's children, will make mistakes. But you can choose what to emphasize. You can emphasize all the mistakes they've made, or you can emphasize the things they did well, and save the lecturing for a truly serious or life-threatening mistake. Your job as caregivers, first and foremost, is to treat them as blessings that God has bestowed upon you for a reason. It's all a matter of finding that purpose for yourself.

Rejoicing the Child

What's in a Name?

When a child is born, you should pick a name for them that represents all that you hope they will become. In *Genesis 21*, Sarah and Abraham had wanted a child together their whole lives, but it wasn't until Abraham was 100 years old, and far too old for a baby, that they got one. They could have been bitter or resentful of God's timing, but instead, they chose to be thankful for this precious blessing. And so, guess what they named their son? "Isaac," which means "laughter." As Michael Card says in his song titled, "They Called Him Laughter," "*This miracle baby they'd wanted for years would make a Messiah who'd give us impossible joy . . . they called him Laughter, for no other name would do.*"

So you see, the things that you say to and about your children need to be filled with joy, because they become what you call them. In *Genesis 32:27-29*, God changed Jacob's name from "heel-grabber" or "con man" to "Chosen of God" or "Special to God." All his life, prior to that day, Jacob had lived up to the name that his mother had given him. But once God gave him a new name, He tells him that this is his new destiny. This is who he is now. And from then on, that is how Israel lived his life.

We too are given a new name when we become a Christian. We're given a new purpose, a new calling, a new way of looking at life, and it's all based on what He calls us. When we go from being unsaved sinners to adopted into the family of God, we become prophets, priests, princes, and princesses in the eyes of God. We're all family.

Children Are Our Heritage

I love the verse from *Psalm 127:3-5* that says, "Children are a heritage from the Lord, offspring a reward from him. Like arrows in the hands of a warrior are children born in one's youth. Blessed is the man whose quiver is full of them." Do you truly believe that? I do. Your children and your grandchildren are a gift.

It is through them that we pass down our values and traditions. As we rear them and teach them, we tie them to the past and all of the family members that have come before them. Likewise, we tie ourselves to the future, ensuring that our memories will live on long after our bodies have returned to dust. It is in this way that children are our heritage. We all battle against the erasure of time. Without children, our lives on Earth would be relatively meaningless. We are physically alive but for a blink of an eye, but through our children, our beliefs, accomplishments and dreams can live much longer than we do!

So what kind of legacy do you want to leave? You can't control where your arrows fall, but you can ensure that they are made from quality materials, that they are crafted well enough to pierce almost any target, that they fly straight and true.

You might say that your child has been in too much trouble, been too damaged, put you through too much to ever be anything but a problem. But I've been where your child has been. (And, probably, so have you.) I've made mistakes. I've caused headaches and heartaches. And God still calls me His child. He still says I am good. And He's glad to have me. He didn't send His only son to sacrifice himself on the cross just to let my friendship go because I'm imperfect. And you can't give up on your children, your heritage, just because they have gone astray.

After all, if we are honest with ourselves, we don't always live as perfect, shining examples of the parents and grandparents we could be. Ask yourself, how skilled of an archer are you? How well did you prepare that arrow to go into battle? How well did you fire that arrow? When it gets where it's going, all alone, will it know what to do?

Until we can answer all of those questions in the affirmative, we shouldn't judge our children because they aren't "there" yet. They are still finding their way in life. It might take them a while to hit their mark, but with you by their side, constantly readjusting and reaiming them, they will eventually learn to fly well and true.

Rejoicing in What We Have

Consider the Parable of the Rich Fool *(Luke 12:13-21).* Two brothers were squabbling over their inheritance, and they wanted Jesus to be their arbiter. But Jesus refused, and instead said to the crowd, "be on guard against all kinds of greed. Life does not consist in the abundance of possessions."

That is such an important lesson in a materialistic world such as the one we live in today. We live our lives to such excess. We want the newest phone. We want the best car. We want the biggest house we can afford. We want and we want and we want. It's sickening. Remember what our Savior said to his disciples? "It is easier for a camel to go through the eye of a needle than for someone who is rich to enter the kingdom of God" *(Matthew 19:24).*

In the end, wouldn't you rather die

surrounded by the people who loved you and not a pile of possessions that cannot comfort you in the afterlife? Some of the most miserable people that I've ever known in my life had big houses and fancy cars. Some of the happiest people I've ever known in my life had nearly nothing.

This lesson really hit home with me the first time I went on a mission trip, long before I had any kids. I flew down to Trinidad, and I was invited to a couple's house that was far within the jungle. So we took a taxi cab as far as we could, got out, and started walking this jungle trail. We went back, back, back up into the hills. It took us a long time, and the whole way there, the man was thanking me for coming to visit his house and his family. So we were walking up this trail, we finally see this little clearing, and right in the middle of it, there's a two room cinder block house with no glass in the windows.

There were some banana trees, some other fruit trees around, and a little vegetable garden off to the side. His wife told him to show me the garden while she fixed our dinner. So, we walked around where he'd cleared back the jungle and was growing vegetables. This was food that his family relied on for their meals. Mind you, it was not a very big garden. Quite honestly, I'd seen better looking plants in people's flower beds or little buckets on people's porches, but I didn't say anything. He was so proud of this place.

He told me to come inside, so we went into his humble home. Truly, it was smaller than most studio apartments. It was barely larger than a garden shed. The "bedroom" was little more than a bed shoved into one corner of the home, the "kitchen" was a camping stove that ran on a small propane bottle, and all their water was brought up in jugs (by hand) all the way from the standpipe on the side of the road where the taxi had originally dropped us off. No electricity, no running water, and no glass (or screen wire) in the windows.

As we were walking back towards the house we could see his wife through the window for a moment. I saw her doing something at the counter, and I distinctly remember that there were tears dripping down her cheeks. As we went around to the front of the house and entered the room, I heard her softly singing. She was singing a song that my church has in our songbook to this day. The song goes like this: "lest I forget Gethsemane, lest I forget thine agony. Lest I forget thy love for me, lead me to Calvary." Her quiet faith moved me then, as it does still to this day when I think back on that trip and that family.

She carefully made me a plate, and as I sat

down, she brought it over to me. Keep in mind, these people are desperately poor. And yet, she served me a full-sized pork chop with plenty of rice. By American standards, it might have seemed like a fairly average portion, but I knew that this was a generous sized plate in this area of the world. Nobody else had a plate, they all stood there and watched me eat.

I learned later that this is a common thing for the very poor people to do in that part of the Caribbean islands. They feed the guest the best portion first, and, whatever's left gets shared by the rest. Wanting to be respectful and show my gratitude to my hosts, I carefully ate every grain of rice and every scrap of meat off of that pork chop.

After I finished, I handed her my dirty plate to take away. She looked at the pork chop and looked at me, and I could tell by her face that I had done something wrong, but I had no clue what it could have been. When she thought I wasn't looking, she took the pork chop bone and cut something off at that little half circle at the top of the bone. I had not eaten the little piece of meat wedged in the top of the bone. So, not wanting to embarrass me, she turned around, cut it out, and put it into the rest of the rice for someone else to eat later.

All that evening, they were so very proud and thankful that I had chosen their house to visit. They were grateful that I let her cook for me and that I allowed them the opportunity to give me the best plate they had to offer. It was an overwhelming experience for a guy that was in his early 20s.

I had never before in my life experienced anything like the joy that I witnessed and felt on that day. They had so little, but everything that they had, they treasured. In contrast, we Americans tend to have more than most, and yet we struggle to find happiness in our lives. That is because joy is not tied to what we own or the things we have. The kind of joy I felt in that room can only be found when we celebrate our blessings and nourish the love we have for our family and for our Lord.

Rejoicing and Traditions

We normally associate celebration with tradition, but here's where we need to be careful. The Bible cautions us about holding fast to tradition for the sake of following tradition. "Why do you break the command of God for the sake of your tradition?" *(Matthew 15:3)*. In other words, if there are traditions that are not based in love for our fellow man or for God, then they are not traditions that need to be followed strictly. It is the spirit of the law, not the letter of the law that matters. Just because it's how something has usually been done doesn't mean that's how it must be done.

Let's talk about one of the traditions that I have with my church family: songbooks. Do you think there's a verse in the Bible that says what kind of songbook you should and should not use? Of course not! The Bible is thousands of years old and has been translated into hundreds of different languages and versions. But the songbook we use in worship is not nearly that hallowed or ancient.

And yet, there were people in our church that were upset when we first started using a projector to show the words on a screen instead of using the songbook we had always used. In fact, I've known churches that split because they couldn't agree which songbook to buy and use. It hurts my heart to hear of stories like that.

That's not what church should be about. Church should fill you with joy and love for the Lord, not fill you with dread because someone wants to nitpick how that love should be seen and heard. The kind of people that want to argue about petty things like that are the people that Jesus spoke of, "'these people honor me with their lips, but their hearts are far from me. They worship me in vain; their teachings are merely human rules'" *(Matthew 15:8-9).*

But that's not to say that all traditions are inherently bad. As long as the tradition is filled with joy, then it is close to the heart of God. One of the traditions that my family had when our kids were young was to watch the movie "Monty Python and the Holy Grail" for Thanksgiving. It is a silly movie, but it brought us happiness and it brought us together as a family, so we upheld the tradition for several years.

For Christmas one year, while following our tradition of watching crazy Christmas movies. I found out that my new daughter-in-law had never seen the movie "Joe Dirt." It is kind of an off-color film, but my kids think it's hilarious. So, of course, my kids insisted their new sister-in-law watch it with them.

The point is, my family has a tradition of having a crazy, twisted sense of humor. The things that we laugh at with each other, the jokes that we tell, and the movies that we watch, might make other people look at us strangely. They might say that a minister's family shouldn't be watching or saying those kinds of things. And they might be right. But it's harmless in the grand scheme of things. It's a way for us to rejoice, and it's not causing anyone else pain.

When the whole family gets together, we tell stories about each other, we joke with each other, and we say things we know will make each other laugh. There's not any of those quiet awkward silences that many families sometimes have. It's just the opposite. It's like the roar of a freight train coming through a tunnel.

As the kids got older and began having kids of their own, we started going to their houses sometimes for the holidays. And guess what? They kept many (not all) of those traditions going. Did they do that because we yelled at them for not doing it? Because we forced them to do it every year? No. They did it because it brought their family joy, just as it brought my family joy for years. Your family should find what brings you joy and do those things together. You don't have to follow my traditions, you just need to have some good, clean fun as a group. That's a big part of what makes life worth living.

So as parents and grandparents, one of our jobs is to learn how to teach kids to celebrate correctly— without getting drunk or doing drugs or any other harmful activities. Because you should never celebrate something in a way that will cause regrets in the morning. This means that, just like any other aspect of their life, we need to embody what we want them to internalize and imitate. In other words, you need to "train yourself for godliness; for... godliness is of value in every way, as it holds promise for the present life and also for the life to come" *(1 Timothy 4:7-8)*.

We need to fill our lives (and the lives of our children) with joy, and then celebrate and appreciate that goodness. And we need to show them the things that are worth celebrating. It's one of the things that successful families (and successful church families) do well. In this way, we will "fan into flame the gift of God, which is in you.... For the spirit God gave us does not make us timid, but gives us power, love and self-discipline" *(2 Timothy 1:6-7)*.

Prayer

Father, thank you for making life good. Thank you for giving us the ability to overcome adversity. Thank you for promising us that even bad things will work for our good.

We pray that you will give us hope and strength. May we look to you for guidance and comfort when things are going badly, and may we have confidence that you mean what you say when you say you will protect us and provide for us.

We ask you to forgive us for the times we're

not faithful. Forgive us for the times when we're greedy or too focused on the future -- too focused on our things instead of our blessings.

May we raise our children and grandchildren to enjoy life. May they grow up enjoying being alive and doing things worth celebrating. These things we pray in your Son's name. Amen.

ROCKS FOR FAMILIES

"The truth is that from the day we're born until the day we die we need to feel held and contained somewhere.

We can let go and become independent only when we feel sufficiently connected to other people."

-Ron Taffel

Rock 5: Relationships — Am I Loved?

We need to make our homes a place of bonding, connection, kinship, association, and networking. Families that successfully raise kids and grandkids have deep connections with each other, as well as with others who are outside of the family.

These deep relationships are so precious and vital. Family members find that they are synchronized in goals, in traditions, and in attitudes. That deep sense of connected relationship is not there with less successful families.

It's also one of those things that's sometimes difficult to talk about. But, if you've experienced both sides of it, or seen both sides of it, then you know what I'm talking about. And you know how crucial it is that families build these connections, both among themselves and with people outside of the family unit.

Here's why relationships are so important: *We can't let go and become independent until we feel sufficiently connected to other people.*

When our "baby" turned 21, he was a senior in college, and we loved telling him "Fly little bird, fly -- make us proud!" And he did, while many others his own age didn't. Why was he able to do what so many others could not do?

When I was a youth minister, I used to tell teenagers that, despite what they might have thought, their parents didn't want them to live at home for the rest of their lives. Their parents wanted them to have a life, be able to make good choices, have the freedom to pursue their interests, be able to drive, have money to spend, and be able to spend time with their friends. *But not until they have built the connections and the support systems that will help them survive life outside the nest.*

And it doesn't change when we're adults either. As parents and grandparents, we need to be able to rely on people, inside and outside of the family. In addition to helping build a family of well-connected members, we also need to be able to blow off steam with our friends or have interests outside of the family's activities. We should have time to ourselves where we can just have a conversation with God and strengthen that spiritual relationship. But if we don't make the effort to maintain connections and friendships, especially after we have children, then we can end up feeling very stressed, lonely, and overwhelmed.

Bonding with Our Children

As with any family, sometimes we feel those connections getting stretched across time and space. But it's the connections that make things work well, so that's why it is vital to maintain them.

There is an interesting passage that I found in the Bible from the Minor Prophets. At the end of the Book of Malachi, the prophet says that, when the Messiah comes, "He will turn the hearts of the parents to their children, and the hearts of the children to their parents." And he says, if that doesn't happen, "or else I will come and strike the land with total destruction" *(Malachi 4:6)*.

It struck me as telling that it does not mention turning our hearts to our mothers, or our mother's hearts towards us. Aside from the fact that the Bible encourages men to play a strong leadership role in their family, I started noticing that one of the differences between fathers/grandfathers and mothers/grandmothers is that the women don't usually need to be reminded to think of their children.

For women, society tends to place the majority of the burden of child-rearing on their shoulders. Women are more likely to sacrifice their jobs to stay at home. Women are more likely to gain custody of children in the event of divorce. We tend to see single mothers more than single fathers. I could go on, but you get the idea.

So, it's interesting to me that one of the roles of the Messiah is to build and reinforce the connections between fathers and their children. Back in the 1980s, James Dobson produced a video series called "Turn Your Heart Toward Home." It was very helpful to us. We were young parents at the time, and he was talking about the things that you have to do inside your family relationships to be successful in the future.

Ultimately, if we don't find ways to turn our hearts towards each other, then we shouldn't be surprised if others don't care what our values are, don't value our opinions, or don't bother to keep in contact after they've left the home.

I see this a lot in families where a marriage turned sour and ended in a contentious divorce. There is nothing more tragic to me than when parents turn their hearts against each other and attempt to poison the hearts of the children against the other spouse. You've got to keep in mind that you are a team, and that even if the love fades away from your marriage, you must never lose the respect between the two of you.

Why? Because your children feed off of that negative energy, and they could begin to turn their hearts away from both of you.

How God Bonded with Israel

We are all God's children, right? So, in order to be spiritually fulfilled, we have to build a relationship and nurture a connection with God. But it is not a one-sided thing.

There is a beautiful poem in *Hosea 11:1-4* that describes the things that God did to strengthen his relationship with the people of Israel. So if you think about it, this passage makes the perfect metaphor for what a relationship between fathers and their children should be. Mothers too, of course, but mothers seem to have a more natural instinct to build that connection, *so ladies, we'll just assume you've got it under control.*

God says, "When Israel was a child, I loved him." I love how straightforward and honest God is here. There's still some stigma these days that "real" men shouldn't be openly affectionate with their children or frequently tell them that they love them. That is a silly idea that we as a society have got to get rid of. Our children (boys or girls) should be able to tell us that they love us freely.

They should know, without a doubt, that Mom, Dad, Grandma, or Grandpa love them from the bottom of their hearts. If God is not ashamed to tell us of His love for us, then why should we behave any differently?

He also says, "I called my son." In other words, He claims us as his, without question, and does not hide his affection for us. One of the things I've always tried to do with my boys especially, is to walk up to them when they are with a group of people, put my arm around them, and say, "You know this is my boy?" For some reason, it always makes them stand a little taller and smile a little wider. It doesn't take much to let your kids know you love them.

Be proud to call them yours, and show them off, even if your kids say it's embarrassing. Because secretly, they feel that connection deepening with every sappy word you say.

And we should be proud of our children, regardless of the mistakes that they have made. My children have made many, many mistakes growing up, but I still wouldn't trade yours for mine. I'd still carve the lung out of my chest to give to one of them if they needed it. So we shouldn't be bashful about those things.

The third verse mentions that it was God,

127

"who taught Ephraim to walk." I love that. Fathers should be just as involved as mothers, during those early days especially. You have so much that you can teach your child. Think about all of the connections you can form and memories you can make just by spending time with them and helping them learn something new.

Also, think about the rest of what He says, "I took them by the arms, but they didn't realize it was me who healed them." To me that means that, if fathers want to turn their children's hearts toward themselves, then they need to be the kind of parent kids can turn to when things get rough. Instead of kids falling down and running only to Mom to kiss their boo-boos or fix their skinned knees, it would be wonderful if kids could run to whichever parent was closest. But sadly, that's not always the case.

A buddy of mine, years ago, was a prison chaplain at the big penitentiary in Parchman, Mississippi. They decided one year that they would arrange for the local Hallmark salesperson to donate some cards for Mother's and Father's Day. When it came time for Mother's Day, they had two big boxes of cards for Mother, and there were no cards left by the end of the day. The boxes were completely empty. These hardened, lifer, gang-member prisoners scooped up all the cards and sent them all to their Mommas.

Then Father's Day came around. Another set of two boxes full of cards appeared. Only this time, they didn't empty either box. Most of the prisoners said, "I don't even know who my dad is." Some of them said, "Well, I'm not sending a card to my dad. He's never been there for me. What's my dad ever done for me?"

That's a disgrace. Our children and grandchildren ought to be deeply and irreversibly connected to our hearts. You teach them to walk. You help them when they cry. You lead them with "cords of kindness." For some reason, lots of men are under the impression that they have to be abrupt and rough with their children. They mistakenly believe that everything they do has to be to toughen them up.

Listen, there's plenty of time when they are older to teach them lessons about toughness and perseverance. You've got to be there from the get-go, holding their hands, giving them kisses, and telling them all the time that you love them so much. Find out what kind of personality they have and what makes them feel happy.

Some kids at my church enjoy being greeted with a headlock, a noogie, and a couple questions about how their life is going. Other kids just enjoy a firm handshake and a smile. Get to know all of the kids in your life as the individuals they are. Shower them with love and acts of kindness.

The last verse of the Hosea poem says, "to them I was like the one who lifts a little child to the cheek. I bent down to feed them." This to me beautifully describes what God does for us and how he feels about us. But it is also a model for fathers. Yes, we should provide for our family, but that means providing for all aspects of their welfare. It is not Mom's job alone. We all should nourish our children spiritually and emotionally, not just worry about their physical well-being.

4 Ways to Communicate Our Love

Learn to Listen

We build a connection to people through the things we do to/for them, and the things we say to/about them. *Proverbs 10, Proverbs 17,* and *Proverbs 21* all say we should listen more than we speak. That is excellent advice, especially when we are raising children. If you are always talking and never listening, if it's always about what you want and what you're interested in, then you risk steamrolling or alienating your children.

When you listen to someone, you should

listen and truly think about what they are saying to you. If you are just waiting for your turn to speak, it makes people feel dismissed and devalued. People can sense when you aren't genuinely interested in their thoughts.

Children are especially sensitive to this kind of thing. If you ask them about their day and then proceed to tune them out and only listen with half an ear, all you are doing is pushing them away. But if you take time to lock in, give them your undivided attention, and truly listen, then your loved ones will return that love in kind.

Proverbs also says that we should be thoughtful and gentle in our speech. This is something I really struggle with, because I love to pick on people, pull pranks, and tell jokes. My favorite game in church is turning the crosses on the communion covers, ever-so-slightly, so that they are crooked, and waiting to see how long it takes for it to drive someone crazy. Usually, by the beginning of the first song, someone has "fixed" it. I like doing that kind of thing. That's just part of my nature. But it's also part of my nature to take those things too far sometimes.

Sometimes I tease too much. Sometimes I'm not serious when I should be serious. Sometimes I don't give things the serious consideration that they deserve. Sometimes I hurt people's feelings.

And that's something I need to work on, because it can push people away instead of binding them closer to me. That's an area where being a better, closer listener can be a big help in my communication with others.

Honor Their Trust

We should be very careful not to betray trust when we're told things. I tell my wife things that I would be mortified if she were to spread around town. If I knew she was going to do that, I wouldn't tell her. Likewise, if I felt harshly judged by my wife, then I wouldn't ask her for advice because it wouldn't be worth it.

Children are just as intuitive. If they come to you with a mistake, and you ask them how they could have been so stupid as to do something like that, then guess what's going to happen the next time they mess up or make a choice that they regret? That's right. Whatever they do, they won't be coming to you.

So you see, there are two elements to creating a trusting relationship with someone you love. *First*, they have to believe that you will not mock them or punish them unfairly. And *second*, they have to know, without a doubt, that you will keep their secrets no matter what. Without both of those things, "the unfaithful are destroyed by their duplicity" *(Proverbs 11:3)*, and you will never gain your children's trust. If they can't trust the promise of your words, then why wouldn't they question the integrity of your actions?

Speak Carefully

Proverbs 13:3 says, "those who guard their lips preserve their lives, but those who speak rashly will come to ruin." In other words, we should work hard at speaking well. I had to get a lot of help from loved ones to learn this lesson.

One of my dear friends was the youth leader at my church for a while before he passed away. One of the things I loved about him was that he was a wonderful listener. If I was upset about something, ranting and raving with angry words tumbling out, he had the ability to sit and listen. He would put the jumbled thoughts I had together in a way that were nice, orderly, and friendly. Then he'd say something along the lines of "maybe you should try saying..." or "Have you tried this instead?"

When speaking with the people we love, we should be careful to say exactly what we mean. Don't say "thanks for coming" when you mean "I'm so glad you're here." Don't say "not bad" when you really want to say "I love you and I'm so proud of you." After all, you never know when you will get the chance to speak to them again.

Similarly, *Proverbs 29:11* says, "A fool vents all his anger, but a wise man holds it back." In other words, we don't have to say everything that comes to mind. Some thoughts are ours, some are put there by the Spirit of God, and some thoughts are temptations from Satan, "the accuser of the brethren" *(Revelation 12:10)*.

Have you ever been watching someone on TV or listening to someone speak and just had a nasty, mean thought pop into your head? That's the evil one trying to sully your godliness. Sure, you could probably blurt out that rude comment and get an uncomfortable laugh or two out of it, but that's no excuse for being a fool.

Remember how I said that child discipline should never be done when you are angry? Well, you need to watch your words as well. If you say something ugly or hurtful to your child out of anger, you are not only crushing their sweet spirit, but you are also driving a wedge of mistrust between you two when you are supposed to be binding them closer to your heart. Remember that even "a gentle tongue can break a bone" *(Proverbs 25:15)*, so a sharp tongue can sometimes do even more damage to your child's psyche than an angry swat.

Practice Patience

As parents, our patience is tested every day. Sometimes, when we are in the middle of a trying phase in raising our children, we feel as if the end is nowhere in sight. We feel that they will never sleep through the night. They will never learn to speak. They will never take our advice. They will never stop hanging out with that friend of theirs that is a bad influence. Take your pick what example you want to use.

But the Bible tells us that we must be patient. *Proverbs 15:15* says that "all the days of the oppressed are wretched, but the cheerful heart has a continual feast." In other words, if we continue to have faith that all things are working for good, then God's words and God's love will nourish and refresh our spirit. Then we can continue to give our children the love and kindness that they need to weather whatever storm they are stuck in.

I'm convinced that sometimes we expect too much, too quickly from our children. Sometimes, we look at kids that are 19, 20, 25, 30, and we're upset because we feel like they haven't learned enough or accomplished enough with their lives.

We're not patient. We expect them to do better than we did, when in reality, we were the same as them. We didn't listen to our parents at times, and our parents sometimes didn't listen to theirs either.

So, what do you do? Do you throw up your hands in defeat? No. You've got to be patient. God will never give up on you, and neither should you give up on your child.

Connecting Through Actions

The way we talk to each other either ties people to us or pushes them away from us. And our actions have the exact same effect. *Psalm 55* speaks of a man who feels betrayed and hurt because he realizes his friend is not true. "My companion attacks his friends; he violates his covenant. His talk is smooth as butter, yet war is in his heart." Here are some actions you can take to bring the people you love closer to you.

Spend Time Together

How much of your day is spent getting together with your family? Now, when I say get together, I don't just mean that you drag the kids out of their rooms and everyone spends the next 20 minutes in awkward silence or staring at their respective phones. I mean the kind of quality time where you are all relaxed and having fun. Maybe it's a little too loud, a little too noisy, or a little too out of control, but it fills you up with that warmth and comfort of knowing you are safe and loved.

In my family, those over-the-top gatherings happen during Thanksgiving, Christmas, and family vacations every other year. We pack everyone together into too small of a space. We share food. We go and do things together. The kids stomp around. Somebody gets tired and grumpy. Somebody screams at the top of their lungs. Something always goes wrong. Somebody has to keep the peace and hug it out. Sometimes kids get skinned knees. It's pretty much utter chaos sometimes.

But there's something special about just being together and building bonds with the people that you love. *I John 4:12* says it nicely, "no one has ever seen God; but if we love one another, God lives in us and his love is made complete in us." If we invest our time in one another, we not only strengthen the bonds between ourselves, but we are also brought closer to God.

Reach Out to People

Jesus spread his love and his healing simply

by touching his followers. *(Matthew 8:3)* We cannot heal the body with our touch, but we can certainly help heal problems of the mind and soul. Casual touch is the cornerstone of any relationship, whether platonic or romantic. Why do we shake hands? Why do we put our hands on people's shoulders? Why do we hug the ones we are close to? Because touch communicates so much. It says that we value each other. It says that we are safe. It says that we are loved. It says that we can relax because we have nothing to fear.

There is a well-known social experiment, conducted by German King Frederick II in the thirteenth century. He wanted to see if children who were never spoken to would develop their own language. In order to carry this bizarre experiment out, he instructed the nurses in an orphanage to only touch the infants in order to feed and change them. Nothing else. No cuddles, no baby talk, no playing with their tiny fingers or their soft hair. Nothing.

It is even more cruel than you can imagine. Frederick didn't get the results he was looking for because the children died. That's how deeply the need for touch is ingrained into our psyche. From birth, we crave physical affection and the feeling of belonging. Without it, we are like ships adrift in a lonely sea.

So if you really want to make a connection with your loved ones emotionally, then you need to establish a physical connection with them as well. Go out of your way to hug your friends, especially those who you know are struggling with depression or going through a tough time. Pat your kids or grandkids on the back and tell them how proud you are of them. Greet your husband or wife with a kiss to let them know how much you love them and are still attracted to them. All of these simple gestures can communicate your love without words.

Commit to Loved Ones

Commitment is communicated not with words but with actions. Can you be counted on? In what situations? Can you be trusted to do what is right when things are difficult?

Years ago, when I got into a pretty serious motorcycle wreck, what got my family through that horrific time was that my friends were committed to looking out for my wife and kids.

When I first came to, the first thing I said was, "Where are my kids? Where is my wife? Are they okay?" I learned very quickly that my kids were staying with a good friend and his family.

Some people thought this friend wasn't what they would consider trustworthy. We used to call him Captain Chaos because he caused chaos everywhere he went.

Several people from my church were concerned that he wouldn't be able to handle it, so they offered to take the kids off his hands. But he said, "No. They were entrusted to me. I'm going to take care of them." And he did an amazing job. The kids stayed with him at night. He took them to school. He picked them up in the afternoon. All of their needs were being met, which allowed my wife to be able to spend all her time and energy making sure I was taken care of and recovering nicely in the hospital.

Another one of my friends made sure my wife was taken care of during this trying time. When she realized she was going to have to be at the hospital for a while, she packed a suitcase stuffed with clothes, several books, and stacks of documents. My buddy who was a pretty muscular guy, was telling me after it was all said and done, "Man, I got tired of carrying that suitcase through the hospital for her."

I asked, "Why on earth didn't you just tell her to leave it in the car?"

He looked me straight in the eyes and said,

"I couldn't do that to her. I just had to suck it up and get it done."

That is the kind of commitment we should all aspire to have for our loved ones. Ask yourself if you are the kind of person who can be counted on through thick and thin. If you can't say that about the people you love, then you've got a big problem. Commitment is key.

Show Grace and Compassion

If we want to raise kind and compassionate children, then we have got to show them grace. The Bible that tells us it is not our job to judge others. "None of us lives for ourselves alone, and none of us dies for ourselves alone. If we live, we live for the Lord; and if we die, we die for the Lord. So, whether we live or die, we belong to the Lord... Therefore let us stop passing judgment on one another. Instead, make up your mind not to put any stumbling block or obstacle in the way of a brother or sister" *(Romans 14:4-13)*.

That is just one of many examples of God's Word telling us to have understanding for the people around us. We teach our children to forgive others and to see the heart of people instead of their mistakes. We do this by first forgiving our children of their mistakes.

When my son broke the church's window, I didn't scream at him for being stupid. I showed him grace and loved him anyway. And, I loved him enough to teach him how to fix what he had broken. It takes a strong person to forgive others, and if we want our children to have that strength too, then it starts with us.

In Conclusion: Start Today

"No one reaches the end of life, looks back and says, "I wish I had spent more time at the office and less time with my kids."

-Barbara Bush

I love this quote. It never fails to remind me of what is important in life. You should always remember that, too. There is no greater gift for your kids than you. Likewise, there is no greater harm to them than the absence of you.

One of life's greatest tragedies is to not be present mentally and emotionally where you are physically. At my church, we're always looking for people, especially in that next generation, that we can invest in and help build up. In this way, we can launch as many arrows as possible into the future *(Psalm 127:4)* to carry on our legacy of kindness and giving when we will no longer be around to do so ourselves.

So I want you to think, right now, about how you can bind people closer to you. Maybe you have kids and/or grandkids of your own. Maybe you're looking to mentor other people's kids and grandkids. Maybe you're thinking about that friend of yours who's been a little down in the dumps.

Whoever it is, be on the lookout for opportunities to connect more or reconnect with them. At the end of the day, your life will feel so much richer for having spent time reaffirming your love for someone. You will be happier. And your happiness will, in turn, make your home a more serene and loving place to be.

Prayer

Father, thank you for creating in us this drive to reach out and build connections with others. We ask that you would help us to be wise and judicious in the way we choose who is worthy of our time and affections. May we do so purposefully, may we do so with wisdom and with your Word.

And God, I ask that you would help us to make a difference in the families we have and the communities we live in. May we always be present in the place and moment we find ourselves in, and may the people around be better after our passing

than they were before we came along. We ask
that you do all these things for us and through us,
Lord. In your name we pray. Amen.

ROCKS FOR FAMILIES

"Carve your name on hearts, not tombstones.

A legacy is etched into the minds of others and the stories they share about you."

-Shannon L. Alder

Rock 6: Tradition — "Where Do I Belong?"

Our home is a big part of our legacy, and it is the birthright of our children. When you leave this earth, your children will use the lessons you gave them to answer the question of where they belong.

People have pondered their purpose and place for centuries. Even the ancient philosophers of Greece sought to answer these things— "Who am I? Where am I going? Why am I here?" When people move, change jobs, change houses, or change churches, it's because they are trying to find where they fit in or belong. Everything in our lives, from the time we were children to now, has shaped what we crave and what makes us feel comfortable, which in turn dictates what kind of place we seek to belong to.

So, if home for a child is a place where Mom and Dad are screaming, arguing, and throwing things at each other, then in the child's mind, they begin to see that kind of environment as normal. An angry home can often produce angry children. That's why you see men and women whose parents were abusive go on to marry men or women that are also abusive. It's a terrible cycle. On the other hand, if home is a loving place where people are caring and giving to each other, then that becomes the foundation for their relationships the rest of their lives. So we want to be extremely careful with the kind of traditions we encourage in our homes.

Our Roots Are Our Personal History

Our legacy begins with our personal history. Right now, our life is like a tree. We will, one day in the future, bear fruit that will become the legacy we leave for our children to sustain themselves. But everyone begins from a seed. Then that seed grows roots. Those roots represent our past. Genetically, there are family traits that tend to get passed down generation after generation. But more than that, you pass down your values and traditions through your children, and they through theirs, and so on and so forth. Ultimately, who you are today is a combination of your ancestors traditions and the choices that you've made as you've walked this planet.

So as you look back on your roots, one of the things you have to ask yourself is, "am I cultivating the kind of fruits, seeds, and roots that I want my children to have? Am I just mindlessly reproducing what my ancestors did, or am I picking and choosing for myself the kind of life I want for my descendants?"

In other words, the actions you take in this life will have a profound ripple effect throughout this generation and the next of your family. For me, I try to be very purposeful and mindful of the traditions I choose to pass on to my children. On the one hand, some things in my family have been the same for generations, but on the other hand, I refuse to continue down the same path as some of my ancestors.

Examining our roots allows us to understand who we are and why we do the things we do today. More importantly, knowing the skeletons in our closets helps us influence the next few generations of our family. Our children, grandchildren, and great-grandchildren will, to some degree, be who and what they are in the future because of how we are right now.

This is not to say that if we have terrible parents that we will be terrible people. God created us with the power to choose whether we pursue good or evil. We just have to maintain a balance in our mind between understanding the past and thinking towards the future. We're not doomed to repeat the past. But if we're not careful, then that's exactly what will happen. On the other hand, we can't be so afraid of messing up the future that we are afraid to live in the present.

Now, there are some parts of the Bible that talk about this idea of a parent's legacy. And I've got to say, that before I began studying the Bible in earnest, there were some passages, like *Exodus 20,* that troubled me. It's a recounting of the Ten Commandments. He says in verse 5, "you shall not bow down to them or worship them, because I, the Lord your God, am a jealous God, punishing the children for the sins of the parents to the third and fourth generation of those who hate me, and showing love to a thousand generations of those who love and keep my commandments."

What's unusual is that there's another place in the Bible where the Bible says the exact opposite— children are, in fact, not held responsible for their parents' sins. Ezekiel says in one of his prophecies that, "as I live, God says, … the soul that sins, it shall die" *(Ezekiel 18:3-4).* In other words, the sins of your ancestors are not your responsibility. So what do we make of these passages where God says future generations can pay the price for what past generations did?

After much thought, I've realized that it's all to do with our roots and what legacies we allow ourselves to uphold. You see, we're not guilty before God for the things that our parents did.

However, if we allow ourselves to repeat the wrong things our ancestors did, that's now on us. If we choose to make the same mistakes that they did, then the actions now become our mistakes and our sins. Does that make sense?

If Grandpa was a mean "cusser and a fighter," I won't answer to God for the fights and the cursing he did. But if I slip into complacency and just follow in his footsteps, then now it's my fights and my cursing that I'll answer for. The question then becomes, "Do I choose what I've lived with all my life, or do I choose to go in a new direction that I've never been in before?"

See, everything in our life up to this point has had an effect on us, whether we realize it or not. We might say that we will never become like our parents, but in the back of our minds, the words that they said and the habits that they practiced have been worn into our brains like water running over a boulder until a path is carved into it.

Without realizing it, we often find ourselves repeating things they've said before, choosing to date someone just like them, or mimicking a gesture of theirs. It takes time and effort to eliminate those influences. So, just as God said, it often takes 3 to 4 generations before the sin of the parent stops affecting their descendants.

So, things that you are doing with your life right now will more than likely still be impacting your great-grandchildren in a few decades. That's why it's so important how you choose to live. That's why it's crucial that you change what needs to be changed here in the present.

Even if your children are grown, they're still following your footsteps. It's like you're in a boat going through a lake. You've got the motor running, and there's this wake behind the boat that makes a V.

Your choices and actions create a wake behind you. Your children and/or grandchildren are like the skiers tied behind your boat. You think you're cruising through life without a care in the world, but then you look back and see the people you love struggling and holding on for dear life.

Embracing Our Past

We all have things in our past that we are ashamed of. Now, I'm not just talking about a little embarrassment; I mean a deep sense of *shame* or *remorse*. It's one thing to roll our eyes when our parents dig up baby pictures of us sitting in the bathtub or with food plastered all over our face.

But it's a much different thing to think about

151

our aunt who was a drunk, our great-granddad who was a moonshiner, or an abusive parent. We might even be the one who has committed a crime or been a bully or ruined a marriage. When we feel ashamed about things in our past, we worry about how it makes us look in other people's eyes. We might live in a constant state of dread or fear that people are going to find out. We might even think that we are doomed to repeat those mistakes and sins. But it's simply not true.

In *1 Peter 4:1-8*, there is a passage that encourages us to leave the past behind. No matter our sins, whether it be "living in debauchery, lust, drunkenness, orgies, carousing [or] detestable idolatry," God judges us by whether we are currently "done with sin" and living "according to God in regard to the spirit."

In other words, the sins of our ancestors don't matter unless we let them matter to us. As long as we stay out of the wake they leave behind, as long as we avoid repeating their mistakes, then their sin will never be ours.

And if the past sins were ours? Well, then, it's in the past. As long as we have truly repented and irrevocably changed our ways, then we can still love and be loved by God.

Similarly, if your children veer far from the

course, it is not impossible that they should find their way back. Do not reject them or turn away from them when they need your love and guidance. After all, *1 Peter 4:8* admonishes us to "love each other deeply, because love covers over a multitude of sins."

A Tradition of Mercy

Raising kids is not easy, folks. They mess up your home when they're young. They eat all your food when they're teenagers. They give you great stress when they're learning to drive. The list is endless.

A friend of mine has a theory. He says that when it comes to raising kids, it takes a set of ruined tools, at least one broken lawn mower, and a wrecked car for each son you rear. That held true when it came to my two boys. Lost hand tools, rusted shovels, ruined mowers, wrecked cars— you name it, it's happened to them and me. I wish I could say I never lost my temper with them, but I'd be lying. But even when I was angry with them, I never lost sight of my love for them or my desire to help them do what's right.

Why not just give up on them? Many times, it would have been very easy to just throw up my hands in exasperation or rage. I could have given in to the urge to walk away and let them deal with the situation themselves.

But it wouldn't have been the right thing to do. You see, I wasn't a perfect child. My dad wasn't perfect, and neither was my granddad. None of us were born into lives of perfection. We were born, and God gave us the power to choose disobedience or obedience, godliness or ungodliness.

Just because you have specific wrongs in your past doesn't mean that you are irredeemable. God finds value in all of us, and he wants us to parent our children as he parents us. "Just as you who were at one time disobedient to God have now received mercy as a result of their disobedience, so they too have now become disobedient in order that they too may now receive mercy as a result of God's mercy to you. For God has bound everyone over to disobedience so that he may have mercy on them all" *(Romans 11:30-32)*.

In other words, God wants you to uphold a tradition of mercy in your family. Now, "show mercy" does not mean "be a pushover." It just means that, no matter what silly or serious mistakes your sons, daughters, nephews, nieces, grandsons, or granddaughters might make, you love them anyway. Instead of screaming or judgment, offer them guidance and support. Instead of turning your back on them, turn your heart towards them. Instead of letting go, hold tighter. When they admit fault or responsibility, be full of mercy in your response. Commit to upholding the promises of our love, just as He upholds His promise to love us, no matter what.

The Legacy We Leave Behind

Preparing for Death

We have to accept our own mortality. Sooner or later, our time on this earth will come to an end. There is a poem in *Ecclesiastes 3* that describes this cycle in such a beautiful, yet simple, way:

A Time for Everything
There is a time for everything,
and a season for every activity under the heavens:
a time to be born and a time to die,
a time to plant and a time to uproot,
a time to kill and a time to heal,
a time to tear down and a time to build,
a time to weep and a time to laugh,
a time to mourn and a time to dance,
a time to scatter stones and a time to gather them,
a time to embrace and a time to refrain from

embracing,
a time to search and a time to give up,
a time to keep and a time to throw away,
a time to tear and a time to mend,
a time to be silent and a time to speak,
a time to love and a time to hate,
a time for war and a time for peace.
-*Ecclesiastes 3:1-8*

Our death is inevitable, so we need to be careful about the legacy that we leave behind. Someday, your kids are going to have to go on without you. I know it's obvious, but it's something that has never dawned on a lot of people because they've just never thought about it.

One of these days, you *will* die, and your kids *will* have to live without you. Shouldn't that affect the way we deal with our kids?

Some parents' parenting style consists of holding their kids much too closely and tightly, giving and doing absolutely everything for those kids. Instead of letting their kids stand on their own two feet and have some responsibility, they never make their kids answer for their actions or deal with the problems they create.

Parents like this never stop to think about

whether their kids will be able to handle life after the parents are gone. If our goal is to give them the easiest life possible, and all of a sudden we're gone, what are they to do? If they are unprepared for when life smacks them on the nose, we've not done them any favors. We've just prolonged the point of agony.

Isn't it better to teach them how to manage challenges and hardships? Isn't a gradual letting them grow up and separate from you more empowering? Wouldn't it be better for them in the long run to let them deal with the consequences of their own poor choices while you're there to keep it from getting out of control?

Yes, we've got to love our children with all our hearts. But we've also got to love them enough to teach them how to live without us. It says in *Ecclesiastes 8:8,* "as no one has power over the wind to contain it, so no one has power over the time of their death." If you died tomorrow, what kind of a life would your children go on to lead? Would they have enough strength of character, knowledge of the real world, and love of God to make it through the dark days that lie before them? That's the scary thought, isn't it?

It's not enough to spare them heartache while we live. It is living a lie to pretend that life will always go their way. Remember, the

Ecclesiastes poem says, there will inevitably be times of weeping *and* of laughter.

We do our kids no favors by sheltering them from everything. But we can teach them to weather the storm patiently and successfully. We can teach them to lean on their family and their church community for comfort. We can teach them to use their faith as an umbrella of protection, to let God's love soothe them long after we have been reclaimed by the dust.

The Power of Story

One of the best ways to teach your children is through stories. When Jesus wanted to leave a legacy behind, he didn't just preach at people from a gilded tower or lecture like a long-winded college professor. He told parables, lots of parables (for example, see *Matthew 13*), and each parable held a valuable lesson for his disciples.

You can do the same for the children in your life. Just like bedtime stories often have powerful lessons for our little ones, it's been my observation through the years that stories older people tell make the greatest difference in young people's lives.

There's an interesting catch though. The people who tell stories because they want to look good don't usually get the effect they're looking for. I've said it before, and I'll say it again: kids are experts at sniffing out the people who are disingenuous. Now, on the other hand, there are people who aren't afraid to tell stories about the mistakes they've made or the things they've said to hurt others. Kids are willing to learn if you put yourself out there.

So if you're an older person and you want to tell stories that are meaningful, you should make sure that your stories are interactive, not lectures, and they should come as a part of being connected in a deeper relationship. You can't pretend to be better than others or all-knowing. You simply have to be open, honest and transparent. There is enormous power in the stories we pass down from generation to generation.

Cultivate a Sense of Belonging

Few things are more important to children than having a place where they feel like they belong, are understood, and are loved for who they are. In *John 13-14*, Jesus could sense that his time on earth was coming to an end. He told his followers "Where I am going, you cannot follow now, but you will follow later" *(John 13:33, 36)*.

When his followers grew concerned, he told them not to worry, that "my Father's house has many rooms; if that were not so, would I have told you that I am going there to prepare a place for you?... I will come back and take you to be with me that you also may be where I am" *(John 14:2-3)*. You see, it is a great comfort to know that you will be taken care of and loved, that you have a home no matter where you go or what happens to you.

So tell your kids and grandkids daily that you love them. Make it a habit to hug them or scrub their heads. Remind them that they are exactly where they belong. Grab your kids by the shoulders and tell them how proud you are of them. Ask them about their passions, opinions, interests, and plans for the future. Just take the time to truly listen to them. What does that do? It helps them understand that they will always have a place in your heart and in your God's heart.

Show Them What to Value

When Paul commanded Timothy to "fan into flame the gift of God," the apostle also remarked to Timothy that his "sincere faith... first dwelt in your grandmother Lois and your mother Eunice" *(2 Timothy 1:5, 6)*.

How does this apply to you? Well it shows us the influence we have over our children. You can make a difference in the world even after you have left it because the world holds echoes of your life when you pass.

Whatever kind of life you live— good, bad, indifferent, caring, uncaring, etc.— is like a rock dropped in a pond. When you drop that rock, when you take that action, when you say those words, there are these ripples that go out, without you even realizing it. Those ripples pass through your children and onto their children and onto their children. Your influence will eventually die out, unless your child happens to drop similar rocks of their own. Then the cycle begins again.

You see, right now, at this very moment, you're dealing with some of the ripples, large and small, that came before you. But the good news is that you can choose to be pushed in a certain direction by those ripples, or you can choose to make your own ripples. You can continue in the traditions of your forefathers and foremothers, or you can pass on values and traditions of your own. Remember, it's what we *do* that matters more than what we *say*.

Be purposeful about what you choose. Be thoughtful. Be prayerful. Be careful. What you set into motion today could launch the next generation or two of your family into the heights of greatness or into the depths of despair.

Prayer

Father God, we ask that you would give us wisdom and discernment. May we be mindful of the things from our past or from our family's past. May we repeat their kindness or work to learn from the errors of their ways.

We ask, God, that you give us the ability to determine how the things that we're doing today will cause ripples and paths in our children's and grandchildren's lives in the future. Please, God, if those who come after us walk in our footsteps, may it be, God, that they will do well and that life will go well for them.

We ask, Father, that you would honor your promise to those who honor their mothers and fathers. We pray, God, that you would bless us and others as we try to lead others down the path of righteousness and godliness. In Christ's name we pray, amen.

ROCKS FOR FAMILIES

"You cannot change your destination overnight, but you can change your direction overnight."

-Jim Rohn

Rock 7: Direction — "Why Am I Here? Where Do I Go?"

We need to make our homes a place of goals, purpose, and intent. All of us have, at one point or another, found ourselves standing at a crossroads in life. Maybe we hate the path we are on but are afraid to take a chance on a new direction. Sometimes we have to decide whether a new job's growth potential is worth risking a temporary demotion. Inevitably, we will experience the profound loss of a loved one and wonder how it is possible to go on without them to guide us.

Whatever the situation may be, we often find ourselves turning to God and scripture for direction. There is a famous poem by Mary Stevenson called "Footprints in the Sand." It tells the story of a person dreaming about their life as they walk down a beach. During the good times of their life, there were two sets of footprints. During the worst times, there was only one set. At the end, the speaker essentially accuses God of abandoning them.

But God replies with the most beautiful thing. "During your times of trial and suffering, when you see only one set of footprints, it was then that I carried you." You see, everyone is happy to thank God when life is going well and the blessings are easy to count, but in times of strife, we sometimes forget that He has not abandoned us, nor will He ever abandon us. He is always guiding us, whether we realize it or not.

And that is exactly what we parents do for our kids. I would move mountains if it meant that I could help my children (grown though they may be) in their hour of need or trouble. My heart pulls me to make things as easy for them as possible. I wish they would never experience heartache or true sorrow.

But we can't realistically shelter them from every hurt and misfortune. What we *can* do is hope that they will let us be present in their lives and allow us to help them through the storms. If we have laid the foundation of a good relationship between our children and ourselves, then, odds are pretty good that they will turn to us in their times of need.

Maybe they won't ask for or desire your help and advice. But, especially when they are younger, you must be prepared to help guide your children in the decisions and directions of life. With a lot of hard work (and a little bit of luck), your children will stay on the path to success long after you have launched them into adulthood, or stopped walking in this life with them.

Examining Our Lives

Self-improvement starts with self-reflection. Before you can help your children move forward on their own journey, you must first look backwards at your own thus far. You must examine your commitments and convictions in life. Are you truly devoting yourself to a life of goodness? Or are you simply content to coast through life making the least amount of waves possible? How are you making the world a better place than you found it?

If there is one thing that God can't tolerate, it's people who are too wishy-washy. In the Bible, one of God's angels tells the people of the Laodicean church, "I know your deeds, that you are neither cold nor hot. I wish you were either one or the other!" *(Revelation 3:15)*. The angel then goes on to say that God is about to reject them for their lack of commitment.

You see, God does not want your half-hearted or empty actions. If you don't believe in Him, then He wants you to honestly reject Him. Hiding, false timidity and making excuses for why you can't devote yourself to Him are unacceptable.

You might think your life is going well enough without God's help, but that's not the way spiritual life works. When it comes to God, you're either in or you're out. You're either with Him or you're against Him. In other words, you need to make a conscious decision to allow Him to work through you and accept that He has a purpose for you, even if you don't know exactly what it is yet.

In the same way, we must make a commitment to our families. You might think that you are doing enough for them by just providing a roof over their heads or food in their bellies. But that's not enough for growing children or a long-lasting marriage.

As I've said before, our children's spiritual and social nourishment is just as important as their physical provisions. We can't wait until the you-know-what hits the fan before we start thinking to ourselves, "Hey, we should be talking about what to do when their friends try to talk them into doing something crazy."

Kids need to understand that different places and settings require different ways of speaking and acting. Behavior that is proper at a ball game isn't proper at all when attending a funeral. Knowing how to fit in well in all sorts of social settings will make them a joy to others and will give them a lead in the "success sweepstakes" of life!

Set realistic expectations ahead of time with your children about how you want them to act, no matter what the situation. And make sure they know that they can count on you to "carry them through the sand" in the hard times.

I know a few parents who tell their sons or daughters to call them if they are ever at a party and their friends were getting drunk. They promise their kids that they won't be in trouble of any kind if they ever made a late-night call like that.

When I asked them why they made such an open-ended promise, they said that they definitely wouldn't be happy that their kids were at a drunken party. But they would rather make a late-night trip than to have their kid risk getting in the car with a drunk friend because they were afraid of being in trouble at home.

That, to me, is a great example of the kind of trust and commitment from us that will help our kids be their best. Make time to have those honest conversations with your children. Make sure they know how to get out of tough situations before they actually occur.

Ask yourself what values and activities you

want your family to prioritize. Just because you have lots of material goods and success doesn't mean that you are on the right path. As Jesus said, "Do not store up for yourselves treasures on earth... but store up for yourselves treasures in heaven... for where your treasure is, there your heart will be also" *(Matthew 6:19-21)*.

I've been to houses where the kids have piles and piles of toys thrown all over the living room floor. No care for the items, no gratitude for the things they have. Everything just gets taken for granted.

In my own household, there were times that we found our kids' rooms, closets and toy boxes to be completely overrun with toys. It was more than they could ever realistically enjoy or even use.

When it became impossible to make their rooms orderly on a daily basis, we knew the abundance of things was not helping them be who we wanted them to be. Having piles of toys didn't make our kids happier than when they only had a handful of toys. We learned that lesson early on.

There were some simple steps that we took to combat this sense of entitlement and materialism in our children, and you can use them too. When our children were very young, we sometimes bagged and stored half or more of their toys and swapped them out weeks or months later. By then, the bagged toys were "new" again.

When they were older, we periodically made them sort through the hoard, choosing less-favorite items to be donated or gifted to other kids. Some of the receiving children were poor, some had lost everything due to fire or general misfortune, and some simply enjoyed having things that an older, admired child had used.

Jesus tells his disciples, "You are the light of the world... let your light shine before others, that they may see your good deeds and glorify your Father in heaven" *(Matthew 5:14-16)*. Talk about high expectations, right? But not impossible ones.

You've got to lead by example. I've said it before, and I'll say it again. What you *do* is more important than what you *say*. If you tell your family, "You guys need to go to church more," but you find yourself hitting the snooze button or making excuses on Sunday morning, then your actions send a louder message than your words ever could.

On the other hand, if you read the Bible together as a family, have discussions, or regularly go to Bible study together as a family, then your children begin to see that this really is important to you, and maybe they should think that it's important too.

If you walk down the godly path first, then you are paving the way for your children to join you later on down the road. Remember, the goal is for them to walk so long in our footsteps that they will know what path to take even after we are gone.

Pursuing God

Walking down a godly path means committing to doing all things with the goal of pursuing God. The sons of Korah are a prime example of just how powerful serving God personally can be, and why we should do everything we can to honor Him.

Several generations before, their ancestor and his followers grew discontented with the role that God called on them to play. Instead of doing their job in the temple with dignity and pride, they complained about the difficulty and grew envious of the priests, who they felt had a more worthy job. As a result, God parted the ground and the rebels were swallowed whole *(Numbers 16; 26:8-11)*.

Korah's sons, however, survived, and, unlike their father, they nurtured a deep sense of love and faithfulness to God in each new generation.

Two of these descendants sang the most beautiful songs about how their "soul thirsts for God, for the living God" *(Psalm 42:1-2)*. Now <u>that</u> is the kind of Godly devotion we should be working towards.

Imagine if we applied that type of dedication to <u>all</u> our relationships and not just the one we have with God. Does your soul thirst to be at home with your family? Do you think about them when you are at work, or do you just put your nose to the grindstone and totally forget about your family?

Sometimes we get lost in the daily grind and forget that we have a family waiting for us at home. The relationships you have with them are a blessing from God and are one of the most valuable things in our lives!

Acknowledge your earthly and heavenly families. Devote yourselves to loving them, bringing them happiness and giving them the best example you can. Those precious connections are nourished as we display the fruits of God's Spirit, which are "love, joy, peace, forbearance, kindness, goodness, faithfulness, gentleness and self-control" *(Galatians 5:22-23)*.

When you treat people according to these "fruits," you build them up instead of tearing them down. You will not only bring them closer to you and to our Lord, but in the process, you also help yourself get closer to God.

Now, I know it's not simple. It's easy for me to just tell you to be a good person, but the truth is that every day is a test of our commitment to building a godly character. There are days when I've been sitting in traffic for over an hour, and I just want to lay on the horn at the yahoo that's tried to cut me off because they think it'll get them wherever they're going a minute or two faster. And some days, I miserably fail that test of self-control.

But that's okay. Because as long as I get up, willing to try again, willing to love again, and willing to look for joy again, then I will not have failed my Father. And I will not have failed my children who are watching and learning along with me.

Pursuing God becomes a journey of self-improvement that will never be finished. While I can never be perfect, God's love for me is perfect. This becomes a life-lesson for our families as well. Our kids and grandkids need to see and learn how to deal with personal failures and successes on life's road. Like us, they are not perfect. They will try and fail often, but in the process, they are loved, and if they are willing to learn from their mistakes, life can get better for them as they go along.

Finding Purpose

In *Matthew 4*, Jesus began gathering his disciples. Each time one was called to serve, they immediately dropped whatever they were doing to follow him. They may have been fishers at first, but once Jesus called them, then none of that mattered any more.

In our own lives, it is not always as easy to hear our calling. I used to be a business owner. But when my business went bankrupt, my second daughter was conceived, and my marriage was at an all-time low, things couldn't have been more clear to me that God was telling me to make a change. It took a huge leap of faith for me to give up on my dream of owning a business. With a little one on the way, I could have just thrown in the proverbial towel and gotten a "normal" job just to pay the bills. But instead, I was drawn back to serving our Lord through ministry. It's now over 30 years later, and I think it's safe to say that being a professional messenger for God has been my true calling in life.

Sometimes, your calling may not be the safe choice. You need to listen to what your heart is telling you, and take a leap of faith. As long as you pay attention to where God is guiding you, then it will all turn out as it should in the end. And once you have found your true purpose, then it will be easier for you to help your children and grandchildren find theirs as well. Here are some ways that you can guide them in the right direction.

Be a Good Example

When it comes to raising children (or even mentoring kids who are not your own), nothing is more important than being a living example of the values you want them to uphold in their own lives. The Bible is full of praise for those who lead by example.

- "In the same way, let your light shine before others, that they may see your good deeds and glorify your Father in heaven" *(Matthew 5:16).*
- "Follow my example, as I follow the example of Christ" *(1 Corinthians 11:1).*
- "You became imitators of us and of the Lord... and so you became a model to all the believers" *(1 Thessalonians 1:6-8).*

Simply put, if you want the children in your life to act correctly, then you need to act correctly yourself. Which would you work harder for: a boss who showed up to work an hour late every day or a boss who insisted that everyone be on time (including them)? You want your kids to do better and be better than you were, but that doesn't mean you are off the hook. You have to hold yourself to the same standards as them, or else the lessons you want them to learn will be meaningless.

Be Direct

I know we want to look perfect in the eyes of our children, but we can't hide our past mistakes from them. Don't try to pretend that you have always made the right decisions or done the right thing. What's most important is what you learned from your experiences and that you are living your life in a better way now.

Deuteronomy 4:9 tells us that we should "not forget the things your eyes have seen or let them fade from your heart as long as you live." Instead, you should "teach them to your children and to their children after them." Even if your past isn't pristine and shining, there are still valuable lessons to be had there. If anything, your kids will respect you more for being honest with them and for having the strength to bounce back from whatever bad decision you made.

And most of all, never be afraid to "bring them up in the training and instruction of the Lord" *(Ephesians 6:4)*. If they have you, a godly adult, in their lives, then they will be more likely to turn their hearts toward the Lord. Doing so will bring them closer to you and God simultaneously. But you've got to start while they are young.

Some people might say that you should let them decide spiritual things for themselves. But never forget that you are the parent or grandparent. You are the World's Best Authority on your kids. No one knows them better. No one loves them more. Ultimately, you are the one responsible for launching them into the world. You know more about what is best for your child than anyone else on the planet.

If God is truly important to you, don't be afraid to proclaim your love for Him or to praise Him for the positive influence he has brought to your family. Just as we require certain levels of performance in the important things like health, cleanliness, or education, I think we should also set spiritual expectations in our homes.

Aside from their spiritual journey, we need to help the kids in our lives make decisions about their earthly journey. We should be there to guide them when they are considering things like their education, future profession, dates, and mates. I once asked a young lady from my church, "what do you want to do for a living?" She answered, "I want to be an automotive engineer." When I asked her how her grades were in high school math, she said, "I hate math and didn't do very well." That just didn't make any sense to me.

So I asked her how she settled on such a math dependent future career, and she said, "My mom has always said I could be whatever I wanted in life." Do you see how a little more honesty and directness from some respected adult could have helped this girl see things more realistically?

Let's be honest, even though we love them all dearly, all our children and grandchildren have different strengths and weaknesses. Some are more book-smart. Some have greater athletic abilities. Others are more loyal or harder working but are weak academically. But all of them need our sincerity, knowledge, and honest advice in order to find the right path for them.

I had a friend who used to be our church's youth leader. Professionally, he owned a set of stores and had computer technology skills. Fortunately for the kids that he was trying to lead, he was also very helpful and direct about their real-world job skills. He taught many how to groom, dress, create a resume, secure personal references, etc. He would do mock job interviews with those who had one scheduled in their near future. His involvement in their lives led to many successful starts in the world of work and earning a living.

Be Careful

In the Bible, the Rechabites were a loyal and steadfast people. God saw how devoted they were to carefully following the teachings of their ancestors, and He praised them for their diligence. He sent Jeremiah to warn the people of Judah and Jerusalem that they would suffer dire consequences if they did not begin to heed God's word as well as the Rechabites heeded the words of their fathers *(Jeremiah 35:1-19)*.

So what can we learn from the example of the Rechabites? It's clear that we need to be careful about the things we are passing on to our children. None of us know when our time will be up on this earth. We could die a day, a week, a month, or years from now. You need to be practicing habits and values that you want your children, grandchildren, and great-grandchildren to live by.

If you were gone today and your children carried on in your footsteps, would you be happy?

More importantly, would their lives be better? Or should you maybe change some things about your life and make decisions differently? If so, then the time to start is right now. You should be able to leave this earth with a clean conscience, knowing that you lived as the best person you could be and that your kids will be okay if they walk in your footsteps and follow the example you set.

Be Faithful

Prayer and faith are such a vital part of raising a Christian family. Building a relationship with God requires time and dedication. Just as your children shouldn't come to you only when they want something from you, neither should they only talk to God when they (or *you*) are in trouble. Teach your children to pray in times of need and in times of happiness. If you model your faith for them, then they can start building their own faith early on in their own lives.

The Bible tells us that we should pray for our children all throughout our lives and theirs. Hannah, mother of Samuel, was barren for years, but when she was "pouring out [her] soul to the Lord" *(1 Samuel 1:15)*, the Lord answered her prayers and blessed her with a son. Even though Hannah had been given many reasons to give up on the Lord and on becoming a mother, she was the epitome of faith and patience.

Sometimes, we get what we want (like Hannah got Samuel), and sometimes we get what God thinks we need instead. If you and your partner are experiencing problems starting or adding to your family, ask yourself if you need to be patient and faithful, or if God is calling you in a different direction (such as adoption, mentoring, or ministry). No matter what path you ultimately take, make sure to walk faithfully with the Lord and speak with Him often.

Pray for your children even after they have come into your lives. Isaac blessed both of his sons on his deathbed, sending up a prayer for their prosperous futures *(Genesis 27)*. And you should do the same for your children. Keep them in your thoughts, but follow up on your prayers with actions. If you want your children to be successful, prayer alone is not enough. Teach them the proper values and model for them how a good person should act, think, speak, and pray. In this way, they will be set on the best path for success.

Your kids may be grown and out of your house, but they still need you to help them, pray for them, listen to them, and sometimes advise them. I think it is so sad when people tell me that they are estranged from their families for one reason or another. Sometimes it was a petty argument over things that don't matter. Sometimes it's just that they let themselves drift apart over the years. But either way, it's such a shame.

It doesn't matter how old my kids and grandkids get, they will always be our babies. I don't think a parent's job is ever truly done. Even after they have flown the coop, you should still be involved with them in your own way. Offer to babysit, make time to talk with them regularly, have family get-togethers. Anything you can do to keep the bonds strong between you will benefit everyone involved. Be there for them in times of joy and in times of need, just as God is there for you. Build their faith in you and encourage their faith in God, so that all will be well.

Prayer

Dear Lord, we ask that you guide us in the direction you have planned for us. We ask too, Lord, that you open our hearts and our spiritual ears so that we might hear you calling us in our lives.

We know that sometimes our own plans are getting in the way of the spiritual treasures you have set aside for us. Let our sight not be clouded with dreams that are not right for us. Let our hearts remain unsullied by greed and resentment.

Let our lives be shining beacons for those little ones who are watching us. I know that all these things and more are possible through you. In Jesus's name, amen.

ROCKS FOR FAMILIES

"As you do not know the path of the wind,

Or how the body is formed in the mother's womb,

So you cannot understand the work of God,

The maker of all things.

Sow your seed in the morning,

And at the evening let not your hands be idle,

For you do not know which will succeed,

Whether this or that,

Or whether both will do equally well."

-Ecclesiastes 11:5-6

Conclusion: God Always Gives Second Chances

Let me close with this story. When I was a youth minister, a man and his wife had one child. This girl was a teenager in our youth group, and she was absolutely adorable. She was cute, bright, witty, and smart. She made good choices and did good things in her life.

Unfortunately, her mother and father believed that since they had produced this beautiful, wonderful child, that all anybody else had to do was to copy exactly what they had done with and said to her. They truly believed this. This guy was an elder in the church and he would brag in Bible Class about what fabulous parents they were and how everyone should be just like them.

The problem is that good parenting is not always transferrable in that way. Families are different. Kids are different. Even siblings within the same family are usually completely different. If you have more than one child or grandchild, then you inevitably find out that what worked with one doesn't always work well with another.

In the end, no one can claim they have all the answers. To me, the *Ecclesiastes* passage above perfectly captures what it is like to be a parent today. Children are works of God, and the Lord is the only one who can truly understand them inside and out. Rather than rest on our laurels or be overly reactive in our parenting, we should be proactive instead.

If what you're doing isn't working, then don't let your hands be idle, just get out there and try something new. You never know what will work. My book is not the end-all, be-all of parenting advice. But of course, I believe it's a good place to start!

So do your best to be a lifelong learner. Be the best person you can be. Try this. Try that. Listen to different people. Read even more books. Listen to speakers from all backgrounds, all expertises, and all walks of life. Attend parenting classes. Ask your kids and their friends for their input. Try learning in different ways. Use the phone, learn it face to face, communicate with email, write letters, take an online class — whatever you've got to do to be better, do that.

That's the best wisdom I can give you.

And so, I encourage you to make sure that you cultivate in yourself, in your marriage, and in your personal life, the kind of good soil that those kids and grandkids need to thrive. Remember, kids tend to become more what you *are* than what you *tell them* you want them to be.

Consider what you can learn from these 7 basic "rocks" that tend to be found at the foundation of most successful families. How can you take what has historically worked for millions of others through history and improve the chances of your and your family's future success?

Give serious thought to who you are. Think about how you live.

Give serious thought to how you can help other parents/grandparents who are struggling.

Remember that God always gives second chances. God can do anything. God can fix any mess that we make, but sometimes He will let us as His children fall down to see if we will get back up.

The only thing that will truly disappoint Him is if we stop trying.

Review:

7 Rocks or Ingredients for Building a Healthy Family

Sanctuary	Provides the place and lets us know we are safe
Development	Provides the virtues and the tools to become
Fences	Provide the context and let us know the rules
Rejoicing	Provides the joy and lets us know that life is good
Relationships	Provides belonging and the proof we are loved
Tradition	Provides roots and why we are the way we are
Direction	Provides reasons and discovery of our true calling

A Cord of 3 Strands

Here's why families and community are needed for the optimum development of a child:

"Two are better than one,
because they have a good return for their labor:
If either of them falls down,
one can help the other up.
But pity anyone who falls
and has no one to help them up.
Also, if two lie down together, they will keep warm.
But how can one keep warm alone?
Though one may be overpowered,
two can defend themselves.
A cord of three strands is not quickly broken."

-Ecclesiastes 4:9-12

Consider these examples of "a cord of 3 strands":

- The Old Testament example of Eli, Samuel and David (Priest, Prophet, King)
- The New Testament example of Barnabas, Paul and Timothy (Deacon, Apostle, Minister)
- Grandparent, parent and child
- Uncle, cousin and nephew

- Elders, ministers and members

You and your family NEED to be a part of a cord of 3 strands!

Prayer

Oh God, we're humbled by the responsibility that comes with children and grandchildren. We're overwhelmed by the world that we live in and the troubles that we're almost certain they will face in their lives. Sometimes we despair, and sometimes we become angry.

But Lord, I pray that you would work in our lives to clean our hearts and minds from within. May we be what we want our children to be.

When they need an example of how to have a good marriage, be a good Christian, be a good employee, have a good job, or make good grades— may they have to look no further than their parents, grandparents, and other adult mentors in their lives.

We pray for our families and for our children. May you bless them with wisdom and discernment. May they learn from our mistakes and keep their hearts open to our teachings. May they make good choices with their friendships. May they overcome the struggles that they find along the way. And most of all God, we want your will to be done. In Christ's name we pray. Amen.

Appendix

Original teaching handout documents that Dr. Janelle uses in his lecture series are available. You can find .pdf version of these documents, as well as other material from Dr. Janelle at: https://www.rickjanelle.com/

You can learn more about Dr. Rick personally at: https://www.rickjanelle.com/about-me-3/

You can learn more about Dr. Rick professionally at: https://www.linkedin.com/in/drrickjanelle/

You can learn more about the church that Dr. Rick preaches for at: https://www.shillingtonchurch.org/

About Dr. Rick Janelle

Who is he?

Dr. Rick Janelle is the lead teaching minister for the Shillington Church of Christ in Reading, PA. He also speaks, writes and coaches others outside of his church family.

He invests much of his free time in the local families and community. Dr. Janelle's ultimate goal is to help younger couples and parents rear the next generation. He does this by applying Biblical truths to modern life and teaching the mindsets and skills that will help children become well-adjusted, productive adults.

What makes him qualified?

- Over 4 decades of marriage (*to the same woman!*)
- 4 adult, well-balanced, and productive children (*along with 4 wonderful in-law ones*)
- Angelic grandchildren (*despite what their parents might have to say about them*)

- 4 college degrees + an ESL adult teaching certificate from Cambridge
- Over 30 years of professional church ministry
- Thousands of readers/students across multiple continents

Where Can I Learn More?

- Dr. Rick Janelle Blog — www.rickjanelle.com
- Facebook — https://www.facebook.com/Dr.Rick.Janelle
- Linkedin — https://www.linkedin.com/profile/view?id=163336114
- Email — rick.janelle@rickjanelle.com

Endorsements

I am more than pleased to recommend Dr. Rick Janelle. I have known Rick for over 25 years and have found him to be of the highest integrity. He is a man who can communicate with and relate to people from any walk of life, and socio-economic level, any education level and any age.

Beverly Stanley Arndt, Bookkeeper
Columbus Christian School, Inc.

I have known Dr. Rick Janelle as a friend and fellow minister of God's word for eleven years. Rick has an in-depth knowledge of the Bible, helping us to dive deep into its true meaning. Since Rick's earlier occupation was owning and operating a construction company, he is now able to relate to his church members in a rather unique way.

Tom Bertolet, General Manager
Bertolet Construction Corporation

Dr. Rick is a very compassionate person. His experience and knowledge have allowed him many opportunities. He is a great listener and has a realistic approach to helping others. His biblical knowledge is vast and from his experiences he is able to explain how God works in our lives.

Rebecca Mauk, Full Charge Bookkeeper
PhytogenX, Inc.

I had the privilege and honor to support Rick a few years ago. He is a man of integrity and great character.

Cynthia Matt
Simplified Administrative Solutions

Dr. Rick has a way with people that is simultaneously calming, encouraging, and inspiring. He asks terrific questions and provides incredible insight. Working with Dr. Rick is one of the most rewarding experiences of my career. I cannot say enough about his character, but there's more to him than being a good guy.

He is savvy. He is smart. He dissects problems and draws upon his myriad experiences in a variety of industries to solve them. If you need a mission-driven speaker or coach to help grow a healthier, family-focused culture in your organization, do yourself a favor and call Dr. Rick Janelle.

Ed Burns
Melior Marketing | TEDx Speaker

Dr. Janelle is one of the most astute and knowledgeable people I have known. He comprehends the human situation, life challenges and makes sincere suggestions to help people and families improve their lives. As a businessman, he possesses utmost integrity and extreme insights.

Harry Stoorza
Animal activist, Consultant, Coach
Author - Paradoxy: Beyond Us & Them

Rick and I worked together on a project designed to improve the health and growth potential in his congregation. I found Rick to be intelligent, thoughtful, and caring. He maintained a great balance; understanding the need for change while acknowledging the natural hesitancy of the congregation. It was a pleasure to work with him.

Claire Young, President
Ignite: Hope and Health

Dr. Rick Janelle is an excellent communicator, an accomplished writer, and someone I always enjoy spending time with.

Doug Edwards, Director of Philanthropy
Church of Christ Care Center

Dr. Rick Janelle and his wife have raised a wonderful family of four, all of whom strive to serve God. He has shared many examples of how he has trained them to be responsible adults, which they all are. If you're looking for someone to speak about how to have a successful family, based in Bible and practical examples, I would recommend Rick!

Cheryl Fischetto, Area Manager
Encompass Home Health

Rick is mature, insightful, and a joy to know. I'm thankful to have Rick as a friend & colleague!

Andrew Cooper
Institutional Retirement Relationship Manager

Dr. Rick Janelle is an amazing teacher, speaker, mentor, and friend. From the first time I heard him speak, I knew that he was different from any other speaker I had ever heard. He has a way of presenting a story, text, or message in a way that is easy to understand, practical, and compelling.

Whether he is using biblical texts, personal experiences or other sources, he is an excellent storyteller and his conclusions are well thought-out. He also has a way of seeing the bigger picture or the overarching message of an experience or event. I have been amazed at his ability to take a seemingly mundane history lesson and suddenly turn it into an important lesson in personal faith with modern-day applications.

I can't say enough about how important Rick's ministry has been to the Shillington church of Christ and to me personally. It is an honor to work with him as his "Ministry Assistant."

Cheryl Snyder, Ministry Assistant
Shillington Church of Christ

If anyone has the gift of influence, it is Rick Janelle. Every Sunday he faces the challenge of refocusing his congregation's attitudes and behaviors. As human beings, we are bombarded every day with non-Christian thinking, and need to be reminded that our transgressions are taking us in the wrong direction. As humans, we are stubborn, and very seldom self-admit that we are thinking the wrong way. Each Sunday Rick faces these sinners and has the task of refocusing their thinking. And, he does it in such a way that most people leave thinking it was even their idea.

Rick's gift of influence is a present that all in his company have the good fortune of receiving.

Bill Bertolet, Principal
The levelUP Group LLC | Capture The Revenue Hiding In
Plain Sight

We as parents, all struggle with questions about rearing our kids. Am I doing the right thing? Should I discipline for this, reward for that? Is my child just in a phase of development? Should I ignore the behavior? Parenting does not come naturally. And the voices of how-to parent and how not to parent are vast and varied.

Dr. Rick Janelle's book, Rocks for Families, lays out a hard-hitting yet soft landing path parents can confidently use for raising their children. This book is a no-nonsense look at the positive growth structure needed for every child, breaking it down into seven easy to understand "rocks" or areas of the child's spiritual, physical and emotional needs. He provides simple and practical solutions based on sound scriptural precepts for healthy growth. Dr. Janelle shifts the focus, however, away from a child-centric approach to parenting, to a parent-centric emphasis and the enormous power parental example plays in the child's life.

Dr. Janelle makes it clear through scripture, that it matters what kind of parents we are so we can inspire our children to follow our example. "A major factor in raising a good 'crop' of children is the 'soil', or the family environment that these kids are raised in. In many ways, the 'soil' we provide is the most important variable. Fortunately, it's also the component that we have the most control over. Where people run into serious problems is when kids can't hear what parents say because the parent's actions shout so loudly."

As a reader of this book, you will come to know Dr. Janelle, as I know him. He stands in the pulpit of our church each Lord's day and teaches from the heart. His lessons are filled with a deep and abiding love for God's word delivered straightforwardly and unapologetically. His love for family, the church body, God's creation and even his dog, Gizmo, are evident in the lessons he presents. Lessons filled with humor, love, patience are always with the purpose of wanting people to know God's love and direction in their lives. Dr. Janelle is a man of integrity and honesty beyond most that I have known.

Wanda Wayne, Postmaster
United States Postal Service

www.ingramcontent.com/pod-product-compliance
Lightning Source LLC
LaVergne TN
LVHW091217080426
835509LV00009B/1036